simply sublime bags

simply sublime bags

30 No-Sew, Low-Sew Projects

jodi kahn

photography by scott jones
illustrations by mark watkinson

POTTER
CRAFT

NEW YORK

Published in the United States by Potter Craft, an imprint of the Crown Publishing
Group, a division of Random House, Inc., New York.
www.clarksonpotter.com
wwww.pottercraft.com

POTTER CRAFT and colophon is a registered trademark of Random House, Inc.

Library of Congress Cataloging-in-Publication Data

Kahn, Jodi.
Simply sublime bags : 30 no-sew, low-sew projects / by Jodi Kahn.-- 1st ed.
p. cm.
Includes index.
ISBN-13: 978-0-307-39362-3
1. Handbags. 2. Tote bags. I. Title.
TT667.K35 2008
646.4'8—dc22
2007051554
ISBN 978-0-307-39362-3

Printed in China

DESIGN BY Amy Sly
PHOTOGRAPHY BY Scott Jones
ILLUSTRATIONS BY Mark Watkinson/illustrationweb.com

3 5 7 9 10 8 6 4

For David, Sam, and Hannah:
With you by my side,
the rest is in the bag.

2

1

3

PURSES and BAGS are the
ideal DIY projects.

introduction

I still remember the first time I went to Cloth World, the fabric store in my neighborhood strip mall. My Aunt Arline took my cousin Mindy and me on a special outing to pick out our first sewing projects. The warehouse-sized store was filled with every kind of fabric imaginable and everything a nine-year-old girl could want: flowery calicos, frilly lace, and a back room devoted entirely to fake fur and felt! In the middle of the store were rows of tables covered with the latest pattern books. Like a seasoned suburban seamstress, I pored through them all—Butterick, McCall's, Simplicity, and, of course, Vogue. I finally settled on an easy-to-sew pattern for hot pants (the first time they were in fashion), then picked out a mod pink cotton print for my creation.

My aunt showed me how to iron and pin the pattern, cut out the pieces, and stitch them all together. We worked at her Singer sewing machine, which she kept set up in the corner of her bedroom. Like magic, those five separate pieces became a pair of three-dimensional hot pants. The seams were crooked and I botched the zipper, but in the end, I had made something out of practically nothing. It was a rush.

I continued to hone my sewing skills using my Barbies as fit models. They had a full wardrobe of gathered skirts and muumuu-style dresses, and a purse to match every outfit. Looking back, I guess that was my first stab at designing bags. After completing my required seventh-grade home ec class, where I made a preppy little clutch out of tan corduroy, piped in a blue and red plaid, I was hooked. My grandma bought me a used Singer sewing machine for my twelfth birthday, and I've been at it ever since.

As is the case with many of life's opportunities, the idea to write this book emerged when I was working on something else. As a writer, crafter, and sewer, I was putting together some ideas for a book on easy style. Like almost everyone I know, I'm usually running from one thing to the next. And although I love to unwind by doing something creative, I don't have the time or, frankly, the patience to tackle super-intricate projects. (The unfinished cowl-neck sweater dress I began a decade ago is still somewhere in the back of my closet.) I admit it: I want instant gratification—or at least pretty quick gratification. That's how the idea for a book on simply sublime style came about.

I wanted to create projects that are loaded with style but aren't fussy or extremely difficult to complete. One of my ideas was to make a bag out of everyday, easy-to-find materials. My quest led me to the no-sew tote you'll find on page 36. Using an ordinary stapler and duct tape, you can whip up this groovy no-sew satchel in about an hour.

As I began working on the book, I realized that purses and bags are actually the ideal DIY projects. They are to sewing what scarves are to knitting: the perfect place to start. With very little investment in time and money, you can add the ultimate personal touch to your wardrobe. And bags are one of the most fun (and forgiving) forms of fashion: Even if you can't fit into the latest silhouettes, or even if the hot new shoes hurt your feet, you can always carry a great bag!

The chapters in this book are organized by category (make-up bags, evening bags, and so on). Each project includes a list of supplies needed and is accompanied by a no-sew or low-sew icon. A special "Green" icon highlights bags that can be made by recycling other materials. The bags are also rated on a difficulty scale of 1 to 5. But don't let those 5s throw you. Whether you're a serious sewer or an eager beginner, my hope is that the projects will serve as jumping-off points for your own designs and creativity. Bags are easy to customize because they don't have to be tailored to fit, the way a dress or pair of pants does. So if you like the shape of one bag and the handle of another, combine the ideas or add elements of your own. Feel free to improvise and—most important—have fun! The results will be simply sublime.

icon key

 NO-SEW That's right; you can make your own designer bag without threading a needle or sewing a single stitch.

 HAND-SEW Sometimes the old-fashioned way works best: These projects are easily completed with a little hand-sewing.

 LOW-SEW Just stitch and go—use your sewing machine or a needle and thread to whip up these creations.

 RECYCLE Repurpose an old item into a new, unique, and eco-friendly design!

project skill level

LEVEL 1 For home-ec dropouts; little time and materials required.

LEVEL 2 Still easy as pie, with some basic skills introduced.

LEVEL 3 Get your craft on without tearing your hair out: These projects will take just an hour or two.

LEVEL 4 Roll up your sleeves and get out your glue gun: more challenging, but still doable in an afternoon.

LEVEL 5 *Project Runway*, here I come! Heavy crafting ahead, but don't be scared—you can do it!

supply closet

Most of the bags in this book can be made with very few supplies (scissors, pins, a tape measure, a stapler, duct tape, sewing machine, and thread). But if possible, it's worth stocking up on some additional items that will make the projects even easier. If you can, set up an area to keep your materials. Even if your space is limited, designate a cupboard or two, or even a few under-bed storage boxes, to house your equipment.

Before you start a bag, read through the entire supply list and instructions. This will ensure that you have everything you need on hand when you begin working. Unless otherwise noted, fabric dimensions are listed as width by height followed by their metric equivalent. For example, a piece of fabric that is 10" wide and 25" high will be listed as 10" x 25" (25.5cm x 63.5cm). Also, if a bag calls for stitching on the machine, you should use a straight stitch unless instructed otherwise, trimming all threads when you're done. Finally, many of the projects instruct you to cover the seams with a long strip of folded duct tape. If you're using 2" wide duct tape (see box on page 13), it will be helpful to make the tape narrower by tearing it down to approximately 1½" (3.8cm) wide. After the seams are covered, trim the tape around the fabric outline to neaten the edges. That's it—now let's get started!

HERE IS A LIST OF SOME OF THE BEST TOOLS AND SUPPLIES TO HAVE AT THE READY:

scissors and cutting tools

Having the right cutting tools will make your life so much easier. Consider stocking the following:

- Good pair 8" (20.5cm) fabric shears
- One pair ordinary craft scissors, for cutting paper
- Second pair craft scissors, for cutting tape
- One pair small, sharp embroidery scissors
- Rotary cutter and a self-healing mat (not necessary, but very helpful and worth the investment)
- Seam ripper (mistakes happen!); also good for punching small holes or making slits

stapler and staples

- Heavy-duty desk model (Swingline is a reliable brand)
- Standard metal staples

show & tell

Make space to hang up some inspiration. I use a coat rack to hang my finished bags and works in progress. Not only is it fun to see what you've accomplished, but displaying your projects can also spark new ideas and keep you motivated. Hang inspiring photos, fabric swatches, and other doodads on a bulletin or magnet board in your "craft corner" (or even on the inside of a closet door). Such visuals will keep you going.

measuring tools

- Tape measure
- Clear plastic ruler to be used with rotary cutter and mat
- Regular 12" (30.5cm) ruler
- Yardstick

glue

- Ordinary craft glue
- Hot-glue gun and glue sticks

pins and pin cushions

- Dressmaker's pins
- Pincushion
- Wrist-style pincushion (I can't live without mine!)

needles and thimble

- Assorted hand-sewing needles
- Embroidery needles
- Assorted needles for your sewing machine
- Comfortable thimble

thread

- Assorted threads (all-purpose, mercerized, cotton-wrapped polyester thread is good for most projects)
- Embroidery floss in assorted colors

ironing equipment

- Steam iron
- Ironing board (for ironing and extra work space)
- Cotton press cloth
- Baker's parchment paper (to use when ironing plastic materials)

marking tools

- Ordinary #2 pencil
- Black permanent marker (such as a Sharpie)
- Tailor's chalk (useful but not necessary)
- Dressmaker's tracing paper (useful but not necessary)
- Tracing wheel to use with wax or tracing paper

sewing machine

- Depending on which patterns you choose to make, a walking foot may be required (see individual pattern instructions)

tape

Although not typically part of a sewing kit, you'll use several different types of tape for the projects in this book. They will be listed as needed, but it's worth gathering these basics at the start:

- Masking tape
- White duct tape
- Clear cellophane tape
- Scotch matte-finish "Magic" tape

task lamp

Having the right light when sewing or crafting is a must. Invest in an inexpensive but bright lamp to supplement overhead and natural light.

sticky issues

Tapes and their various widths—especially when it comes to duct tape—can be confusing, so keep the following details in mind. Duct tape comes in a standard width of 1.88" (4.8cm), which is generally referred to as "2"-wide" tape (one example is Duck Brand duct tape). This width of duct tape is available in a roll of 20 yards (18m)—the "average-looking" roll of duct tape you'll see—as well as rolls of 60 yards (54m) and other lengths. To complicate matters, 3M makes a smaller roll, 1½" wide by 4.72 yards long (3.8cm x 4m). For our purposes, when you see "duct tape" in a supplies list with no width indicated, any width will do. Any pattern requiring the smaller-width tape will designate that width specifically. And even the smaller widths are easily created from your standard roll, because duct tape is simple to tear into strips. Also, unless a pattern lists a particular length measurement for the duct tape, one roll will suffice.

On another tack, clear packing tape that measures 1.88" (4.8cm) wide is referred to as "2"-wide" packing tape. Any packing tape called for in these patterns is this standard 2" size, so no width will be indicated. And as with the duct tape, if you don't see a length specified, one standard roll will do you.

One more thing: When using any kind of sticky tape, make sure to work on a surface that won't be damaged when you peel the tape away. A Formica table or counter or a large plastic (poly) cutting board works well.

1

kiss and make up

make-up bags

Make-up bags aren't just for lipstick anymore. They've become the ultimate multitasker. These zippy little pouches are the perfect place to stash just about anything: tampons, manicure tools, sewing supplies—you name it. My brother uses one made from heavyweight vinyl to store his computer cords and phone charger when he travels. And, of course, every gal needs a make-up case for her purse, one for her medicine cabinet, and another for her carry-on luggage. So let's begin with make-up cases: They're a lot of bag for your buck!

You'll notice that many of the bags in this chapter are similar in shape but made in different ways, with a tweak here or there. The idea is to introduce some of the basic techniques used throughout the book. (More involved techniques will be covered in later chapters.) Although some of the bags are completely no-sew, most of them can also be hand-sewn or stitched up on the machine if you like. In addition, this chapter offers some easy shortcuts for putting in zippers— new ideas that even seasoned pros may not have tried. And don't worry if you mess up—just start again! These bags don't require much time or many materials. Once you master these little pouches, you'll be ready to tackle just about any bag in the book (or at least have a place to store your mascara).

wonder bag

The hardware store is one of my favorite places to shop. On a recent visit, I spied several rolls of clear plastic—you know, the stuff old ladies use to cover their sofas. It came in varying thicknesses and was wrapped in printed tissue that illustrated the many other uses of this "wonder" fabric. I took home a yard (it was less than $10 for a huge piece) and figured I'd make something out of it eventually.

Clear plastic is, of course, the perfect material for a make-up bag. It's waterproof and allows you to locate your eyeliner pencil without dumping out everything else. But sewing it on the machine looked kind of sloppy. Then I remembered how my daughter and her friends liked to play with plastic Perler beads. After creating a design with the beads, you iron them, melting all the edges together to set the image in place. I figured I'd try melting the bag seams together in the same way. You won't believe how easy it is!

finished measurements
2½" x 9½" x 6½" (6.5cm x 24cm x 16.5cm)

supplies
10" x 22" (25.5cm x 56cm) piece clear plastic covering (as thick as possible—16 gauge is best)
Iron and ironing board
Parchment paper or wax paper
Colored snap

1. Fold the plastic in half to create a 10" x 11" (25.5cm x 28cm) rectangle, with the fold at the bottom.

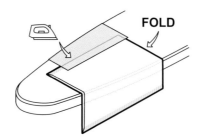

FOLD

2. Set your iron on high. Using parchment or wax paper as a "press cloth" to protect your iron, use the iron tip to fuse the side seams, creating a ½" (13mm) seam. The sides should now be melted together. Allow to cool completely.

3. Make the bottom: With the bag still inside out, flatten one corner to create a triangular point. Draw a 2½" (6.5cm) line perpendicular to the side seam and 1¼" (3cm) from the corner point.

Using the paper "press cloth," iron the triangle. When the fused plastic cools, trim off the point to ½" (13mm).

apart.) Fold the top edge inside to form a 2¾" (7cm) flap. Work the plastic so you get the finished shape you want.

4. After the bag has completely cooled, turn it right side out. (Turning it before the plastic has cooled will pull the seams

5. Add the snap pieces to the center top of the bag ¾" (2cm) down from the top edge on the front and back of the bag, following the package instructions.

6. Personalize your bag with stickers, "punk" pins, or decals. (To make your own decals, see box below.)

make your own decal

Use decal sheets, designed for use with inkjet printers and available at office supply stores, to make your own groovy decal. Using your computer, print a design on the clear side of the decal sheet and let the image dry completely. To keep your decal from smearing, spray it with a light coat of aerosol hair spray. The hair spray acts as a fixative and will protect the image. Cut the decal out, peel off the back liner, and apply it to your bag.

charmed, i'm sure

charmed, i'm sure

The inspiration for these easy bags was a bucket of colorful zippers at my local fabric store. The woman who owns the shop had acquired some really unusual retro shades, such as peacock blue, mustard yellow, orangey squash, and mossy green. I thought the zippers would go great with some cute vintage-looking plastic charms I had found online. For the fabric, I kept with the retro theme and picked some bold, contrasting polyester vinyl, the kind you see on old kitchen or diner chairs. In addition to being waterproof, vinyl doesn't fray, so the edges don't need to be hemmed. You can find vinyl at a fabric or hardware store (in limited colors), or you can hit up your local upholsterer for some scraps. Mine sold me a bundle of swatches for a few dollars.

This bag will also allow you to practice putting in the much-feared zipper. The secret with these bags is to start with a zipper that is several inches longer than the width of the bag (more on this later). You don't even need a zipper foot! But be careful—these bags are truly addictive. (In fact, buy enough materials for at least two or three pouches. After you make the first one, you'll be able to whip out another very quickly.)

You can make this bag any size you want. Just pick a zipper several inches longer than your desired finished width. Dimensions and directions here are for the small orange bag pictured.

finished measurements
6½" x 4¼" (16.5cm x 11cm)

supplies
7" x 8" (18cm x 20.5cm) piece vinyl fabric

Scotch matte-finish "Magic" tape or clear cellophane tape

12" (30.5cm) or longer all-purpose polyester zipper (in contrasting color)

Sewing machine

Thread (to match zipper color)

Charm

optional
Vegetable oil and paper towel or walking (or Teflon) foot attachment

Rotary cutter and self-healing mat

1. Trim the fabric into a rectangle 6½" x 8" (16.5cm x 20.5cm). (Save the trimmed vinyl for a charm pull.)

2. With the fabric wrong side up, place the closed zipper, face down, lengthwise along one of the 8" (20.5cm) edges so that the zipper teeth are approximately ¼" (6mm) *above* the fabric edge. The end of the zipper (slider) should be about ½" (13mm) in from the side edge. (A little of the zipper tape will hang off the edge.) Use Scotch "Magic" tape to temporarily secure the zipper, taping just the very edge of the zipper to the fabric.

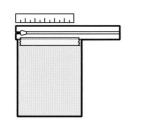

3. Turn the fabric over to make sure the zipper is placed where you want it. If not, reposition it.

4. Open the zipper. On your machine, sew the zipper on the *wrong* side of the fabric, lining up the side of the presser foot with the zipper teeth for a ¼" (6mm) seam. (Vinyl is slippery, so sewing on the wrong side helps the fabric feed more easily.)

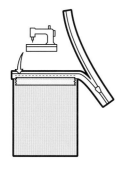

5. Close the zipper, and tape the un-sewn side of the zipper to other 8" (20.5cm) edge, making sure the bag's side edges line up.

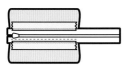

6. Open the zipper, and stitch the unsewn side in place on the other top edge.

7. Celebrate—you've put in the zipper!

8. Remove the Scotch "Magic" tape, and turn the bag right side out. Line up the bag sides, and stitch them together using a ¼" (6mm) seam allowance. Sew all the way up both sides, back-stitching back and forth over the zipper and at each end of the side seams.

9. Trim the edges close to the seams, trimming off the extra zipper length using a rotary cutter and mat or sharp scissors.

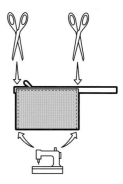

10. From the leftover vinyl, cut a very thin strip, about ⅛" x 8" (3mm x 20.5cm). Use this strip to tie your charm to the zipper. Trim the ends of the strip.

charm school

You can purchase or make any kind of charm to decorate your bag. Try a blank metal dog tag, a cool old key, or a "real" charm from a broken bracelet. Or poke a hole through a plastic Barbie doll shoe or a stray piece from a board game, such as a Monopoly house. Any trinket will do!

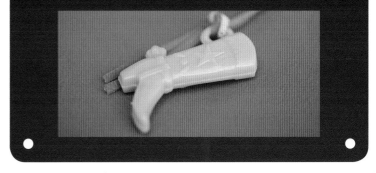

flower power

The first bag I designed for this book was a no-sew tote put together with a stapler and duct tape. I was surprised how sturdy it turned out (the sticky duct tape reinforces the staple stitches) and how easy and fun it was to make. This make-up bag is a mini version of that tote, with a few twists. I wanted the bag to close, so I added a magnetic snap, and I embellished the bag with a flower and a tag. This bag can be made out of any heavy material, such as canvas, patent leather vinyl, or oilcloth. You can even use a shiny shower curtain—just save the leftover material for a bigger no-sew tote later on (see page 36)!

finished measurements
3" x 8½" x 5½" (7.5cm x 21.5cm x 14cm)

supplies
10" x 18" (25.5cm x 45.5cm) piece heavyweight fabric (such as canvas, patent leather vinyl, or oilcloth)
Colored masking tape
Silk flower
Pencil
Pointed wooden skewer or toothpick
1½" wide duct tape (in matching or complementary color)
Magnetic purse snap
Stapler and staples

1. With right sides together, fold the fabric in half to create a 10" x 9" (25.5cm x 23cm) rectangle, with the fold at the bottom.

2. Fold the top raw edges back on the front and back to create a 2" (5cm) hem. Use masking tape to temporarily hold the hem in place.

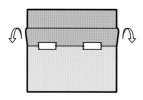

3. Attach the flower: Pull the silk flower off its plastic stem, and remove the green plastic "calyx"—the little base at the bottom—from the back of the flower. Position the flower at the center of one top hem, and mark the spot with a pencil on the right side of the fabric. This will become the front of the bag.

4. Untape the front hem, and poke a hole at the marked spot (only through the front layer, not through the hem allowance) using a pointed wooden skewer, a toothpick, or another pointed implement.

5. Poke the flower through the fabric from the right side to the wrong side. Use scissors to slit the exposed plastic stem in half so that it can be flattened out on the wrong side of the bag. Cover the stem with a small square of duct tape to hold it in place.

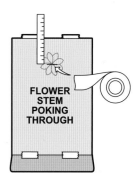

FLOWER STEM POKING THROUGH

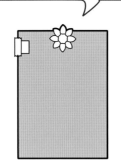

6. Attach the magnetic snap: Following the package instructions, attach the snap pieces to the inside hems. On the side of the bag with the flower, make sure the snap piece covers the back of the stem.

7. With the flower and the snap pieces in place, secure the top hems with duct tape.

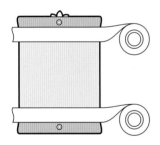

8. Attach a tag: Turn the fabric over so that the material is right side up and the flower is at the top. Place the tag, *face side down*, on the left side of the bag, 1" (2.5cm) from the top edge. Make sure that your design or writing faces in toward the center of the bag and clears the seam allowance. Use a piece of masking tape to temporarily hold the tag in place, keeping the tape in the seam allowance.

9. Staple the sides together: With right sides together, fold the bag in half, using masking tape to temporarily hold it in place. Staple the sides together using a ½" (13mm) seam allowance and removing the masking tape as you go. Make sure the staples are close together to create a clean, straight line. Trim any extra tag material. Clip the top corners on a diagonal in the seam allowance; then cover the seams with duct tape (folded lengthwise over the raw edge).

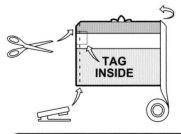

TAG INSIDE

10. Make the bottom: With the bag still inside out, flatten one corner to create a triangular point. Draw a 3" (7.5cm) line perpendicular to the side seam and 1½" (3.8cm) from the corner point. Staple along the line. Repeat on the other side. Trim the seam to ½" (13mm). Cover the seam with duct tape (folded lengthwise).

11. Turn the bag right side out. The fabric may feel stiff and hard to turn. Keep working the fabric, and the bag will take shape.

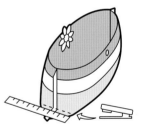

tag, you're it!

Put your personal stamp on your bag or purse by making your own bag tag. Use a piece of grosgrain ribbon, a plastic tab from a notebook divider, or even a colorful piece of masking tape folded in half. Use a permanent marker or a rubber stamp and ink to decorate your tag.

city slicker

Brightly checked and printed oilcloth, made popular as a table covering in the 1950s, is now used for everything from wallets to bibs. (See more on the history of oilcloth on page 27.) The shiny, coated vinyl is waterproof and easy to clean, making it another perfect material for make-up cases. Maybe it's the retro feel or the fabric's slick finish—there's just something about oilcloth that puts a smile on your face.

This bag may look difficult, but actually the hardest part is cutting out the shape. Once you've figured that out, the rest is sort of like an origami project. With just a few folds and seams, you'll be ready to hit the road.

finished measurements

4¼" x 9¾" x 5" (11cm x 24.7cm x 12.5cm)

supplies

31" x 19" (79cm x 48.5cm) piece oilcloth

24" (61cm) or longer heavyweight nylon coil zipper (sometimes referred to as an "upholstery" zipper)

Sewing machine

Thread

Duct tape

8" (20.5cm) of 1" (2.5cm) wide nylon webbing (for strap)

1. Cut out the bag: Fold the fabric in half to form a 15½" x 9½" (39.5cm x 24cm) rectangle. Cut out a 2½" (6.3cm) wide by 4½" (11.4cm) tall rectangle from each side, 2½" (6.3cm) from the top and bottom edges, as shown. (Note, you'll be cutting through both layers.)

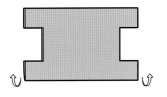

here's the rub

When sewing slippery or sticky material, such as vinyl, patent leather, or oilcloth, it helps to use a walking (or Teflon) foot attachment on your machine. These special feet help "feed" slick or thick fabric as you sew.

If you don't want to bother with an attachment but still find your stitches are clumping together, dab a little vegetable oil on the fabric where you'll be stitching. Like a walking foot, the oil helps keep the fabric from sticking. Wipe away the oil right after you sew to keep it from getting all over. Use a few layers of paper towel to clean your sewing machine foot, too.

2. Put in the zipper: With the right side of the fabric facing the right side of the zipper, center the zipper ⅛" (3mm) below one of the top edges (there will be a few inches of extra zipper hanging off both sides). Pin or tape the zipper in place. Using a ⅜" (1cm) seam allowance, stitch the zipper, guiding your regular presser foot against the zipper teeth as you go.

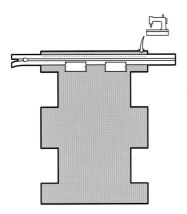

3. Finger-press the zipper back so that it now faces up. Stitch the zipper in place by topstitching close to the edge. Repeat to attach the other side.

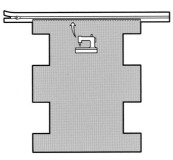

4. Sew up the zipper ends: Turn the bag inside out. Close the zipper halfway, and flatten the bag so that the tab edges line up. (Note: Before stitching, make sure the zipper slider is on the inside part of the bag.) Stitch the tab edges closed using a ¼" (6mm) seam allowance, sewing back and forth a few times over the end of the zipper. Trim off the extra zipper length at each end. Repeat on the other side of the zipper.

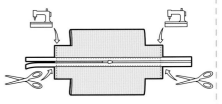

5. Use a thin strip of duct tape (folded lengthwise) to cover each joined tab edge, enclosing the zipper ends.

6. Attach the strap and sew up the side ends: On the zipper end side of the bag, position the strap on the inside of the bag, lining up the center of the strap edges with the center seam (press the seam down flat). Pin or baste the strap in place. Pin the sides together and stitch, sewing back and forth a few times over the strap to reinforce. Repeat on the other side (without adding the strap).

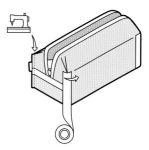

7. Trim the loose threads and neaten up the edges. Cover all seams with a thin strip of duct tape (folded lengthwise), and trim the tape around the fabric outline to neaten the edges.

8. Turn the bag right side out.

what, exactly, is "oilcloth"?

When you think of oilcloth, you probably imagine colorful printed vinyls: red checks, cheery fruits, funky flowers, and bold plaids. But originally, oilcloth was not made from vinyl, but rather from natural-fiber materials, such as canvas, linen, or burlap, and treated with layers of linseed oil to waterproof it (thus the name oilcloth). The fabric was then block-printed by hand with beautiful decorative designs.

Probably first used in China in the seventh century, oilcloth turned up in England in the 1500s. During the U.S. Civil War, oilcloth knapsacks and backpacks made protective pouches for matches and other explosives. In the colonial era, it was used as a floor covering, and around 1910, it became popular as a table covering. The bright retro designs that have been reintroduced today are mostly patterns from the 1940s and 1950s. By that time, oilcloth was made by engraving and printing designs directly on vinyl (a process called *rotogravure*). A clear coat of plastic or PVC was added, taking the place of the oil. Although not technically "oilcloth," the shiny printed fabric we now know as such remains inexplicably seductive and mood elevating!

birthday girl

When I told my next-door neighbor Beth that I was working on a book about bags, she mentioned not being able to find a make-up bag that was long enough for her blush brush (a common complaint!). So I designed this bag with Beth in mind: simple but bold, stylish, cute, and lots of fun. The bag makes up for in width what it lacks in height—at 9" (23cm) wide, it'll hold just about any make-up brush. I gave the bag to Beth for her birthday and personalized it with a tag that said "Birthday Girl" for a truly one-of-a-kind gift.

finished measurements

3⅛" x 9" x 3½" (7.8cm x 23cm x 9cm)

supplies

½ yard (45.5cm) piece fabric (for bag)

½ yard (45.5cm) piece heavyweight lining material (such as heavy, waterproof vinyl canvas or cotton canvas)

Sewing machine

Thread

Masking tape

Personal computer

Fabric transfer paper for inkjet printer (often used for quilting)

Duct tape

Snap

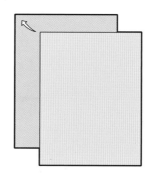

1. From the bag fabric, cut a 12½" x 16" (32cm x 40.5cm) rectangle.

2. From the lining material, cut another rectangle the same size.

3. With right sides together, pin the bag fabric and lining piece, and stitch along each short edge using a ½" (13mm) seam allowance.

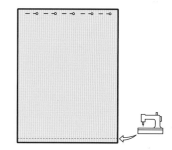

4. Turn right side out and press.

5. With fabric right side out, baste the fabric and lining together at the side seams using a ¼" (6mm) seam allowance. (Hint: The fabric will feed more easily if you sew on the lining side rather than the fabric side.)

6. With the lining side up, fold over the top and bottom edges to create 2½" (6.5cm) flaps. Use masking tape to temporarily hold the flaps in place.

7. Fold the bag in half with right sides together, making sure all edges line up. Stitch the sides together using a ½" (13mm) seam allowance and backstitching at the top and bottom of each seam.

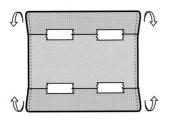

8. Make the tag: Use your computer to design your tag. Print the tag on fabric transfer paper using an inkjet printer. Cut out the tag and fold it in half. Remove the backing paper before placing the tag in the bag.

9. Adjust the side seams: Draw a diagonal line from a point on the top edge, 1½" (3.8cm) from the side, to a point on the *seam line*, 1½" (3.8cm) from the bottom fold. Repeat on the other side of the bag.

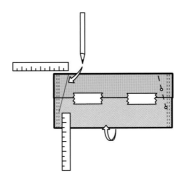

10. Use straight pins to mark the new side seams. Using the pins as a guide, reach inside the bag and position the tag, with the end of the tag within the new side seam at the desired angle. Temporarily secure the tag with a piece of masking tape.

11. Sew the new side seams by stitching on the diagonal (as marked), making sure to catch the tag ends. Trim the seams to ½" (13mm). Remove the masking tape.

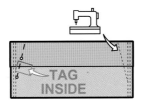

12. Make the bottom: With the bag still inside out, flatten one corner to create a triangular point. Draw a 3" (7.5cm) line perpendicular to the side seam and 1½" (3.8cm) from the corner point. (Note: The side seam will appear slightly on an angle, so line up perpendicularly with the *top* of the seam.) Sew along the line. Repeat on the other side. Trim the seam to ½" (13mm).

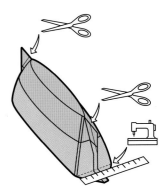

13. Cover all seams with a thin strip of duct tape (folded lengthwise over the raw edge). Trim the tape around the fabric outline to neaten the edges.

14. Following the package instructions, attach the snap to the top center of the bag, about ¾" (2cm) down from the top edge. Turn the bag right side out.

caution!

caution!

No need to proceed with caution when making this super-easy bag: It's completely no-sew (even the zipper is stapled in) and can be pieced together in an hour. The "fabric" is made by layering pieces of "CAUTION" tape over strips of yellow duct tape to create a bag that looks and feels as if it's made out of heavy, printed vinyl. One thing's for sure: This bag will definitely make a statement!

finished measurements
10½" x 6¼" (26.5cm x 16cm)

supplies
Roll of "CAUTION" tape
(available at hardware stores)

Yellow duct tape

Scotch matte-finish "Magic" tape

12" (30.5cm) or longer
heavyweight black zipper

Stapler and staples

Masking tape

1. Make the "CAUTION" fabric: Cut 4 sections, each 16" to 18" (40.5cm to 45.5cm) long, with the word "CAUTION" centered in each. Begin with 1 printed strip, lettered side down. Cover it with a strip of duct tape, sticky side down. Place a second strip of duct tape, sticky side down, so that it overlaps the edge of the first tape strip. Then turn the swatch over. Lay down a second printed strip so that it slightly overlaps the first printed strip and sticks to the exposed tape. Continue laying down printed strips and tape in this manner, overlapping them slightly

and flipping the fabric over and back as you go, until all 4 printed strips are connected.

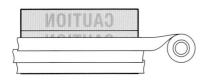

2. Trim the side edges to create a piece 12" (30.5cm) wide.

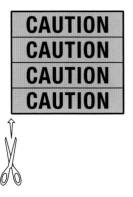

3. Attach the zipper: Place the zipper face down on the right side of the fabric, with the slider end of the zipper ¾" (2cm) from the left side and with the top zipper edge even with the top fabric edge. Temporarily hold the zipper in place with Scotch "Magic" tape.

4. Staple the zipper in place, ¼" (6mm) from the top edge. (Open the zipper, if necessary, to keep the zipper tape flat and the seam straight.)

5. Remove the Scotch "Magic" tape. Turn the bag over, pressing the seam back to flatten out the zipper. Cover the staples with a strip of duct tape. Trim the extra duct tape, leaving the extra zipper length intact for the moment.

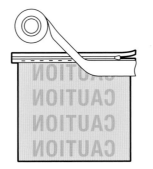

6. Fold the "CAUTION" fabric in half with right sides together, lining up the unstapled side of the zipper with the other top raw edge of the fabric. Use Scotch "Magic" tape or masking tape to temporarily hold the bag sides in place. Attach the zipper to the opposite edge of the fabric in the same manner as before, then remove the tape from the sides. Press

back the seam you just stapled to flatten out the zipper. Again, cover the staples with a strip of duct tape, trimming the extra tape but leaving the extra zipper length intact.

7. With the bag still inside out and the zipper closed, flatten the bag so that the zipper pull is on the right-hand side and the zipper teeth are about 1" (2.5cm) from the top of the bag. Use masking tape to temporarily hold the sides together.

8. Staple the sides together using a ½" (13mm) seam allowance, *opening the zipper* before you staple the second side. Staple over the zipper as best you can, removing the masking tape as you go.

9. Trim off the extra zipper length, and cover the seams with duct tape (folded lengthwise). Trim the tape around the fabric outline to neaten the edges. Turn the bag right side out.

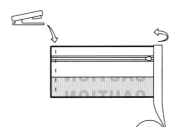

2

easy does it
simple totes

The tote bag you carry says a lot about you—for example, it may tell whether you've recently donated to your public radio station or run a 5K, or reveal where you work or even where you bank or shop.

If this is the case, it's time to dump the logo bookbag, canvas promotional carryall, or paper shopping bag and treat yourself to a cute little tote. Add some style to your daily schlep! The bags in this chapter are so easy to make, you'll want to churn out a closetful. Some are constructed out of everyday items, such as place mats and shower curtains, while others utilize easy-to-find supplies purchased at your local hardware or fabric store. No matter what they're made from, these simple, sturdy satchels are easygoing, hardworking, and great looking.

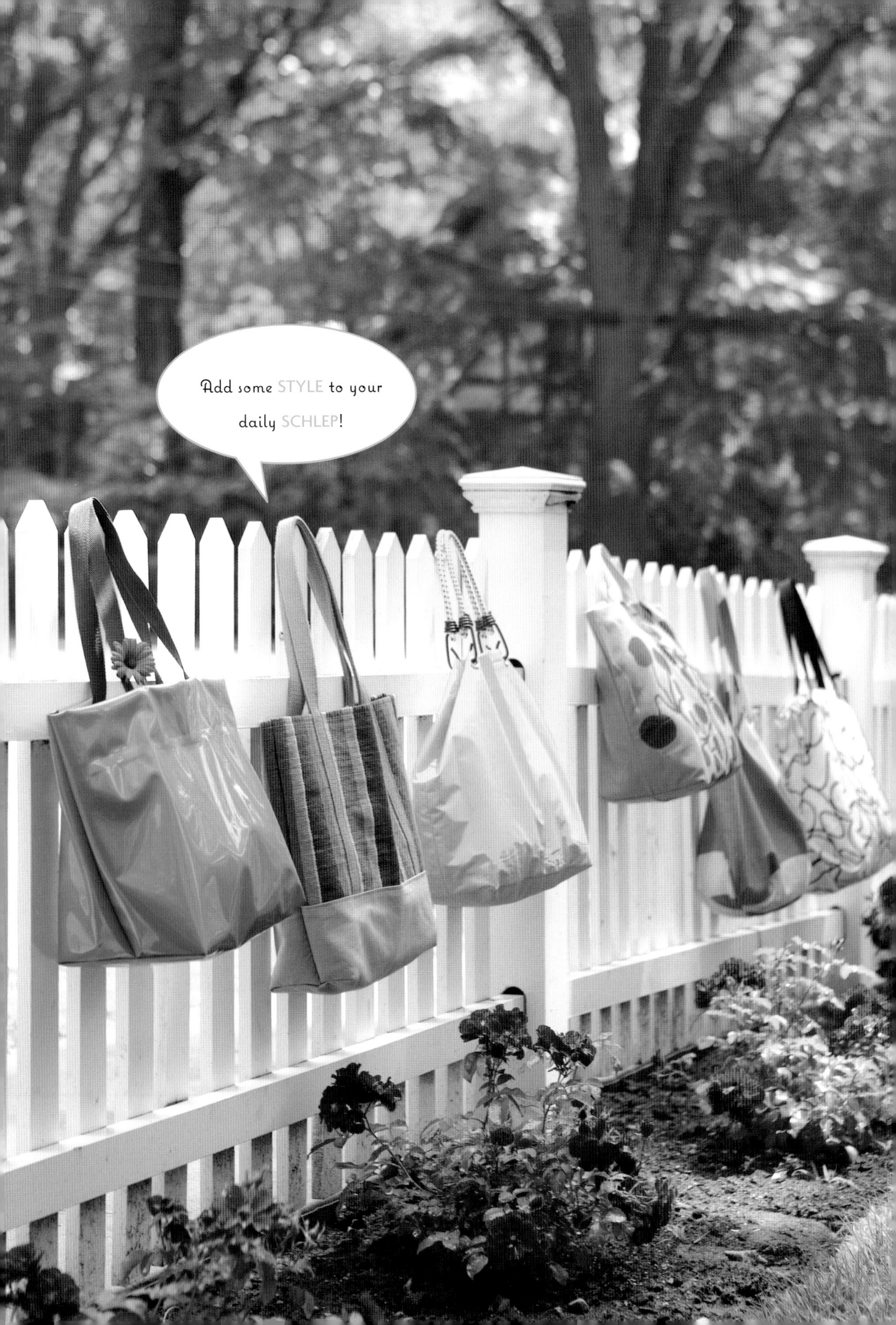
Add some STYLE to your daily SCHLEP!

original no-sew tote

LEVEL 3

The tote pictured here is made from heavyweight patent leather vinyl, which can be purchased at a fabric store or online (see the resource section, page 116). It's very sturdy, waterproof, and much less expensive than real patent leather. But any heavyweight fabric will work. Try using a canvas drop cloth or upholstery material to create an entirely different look.

Like the Flower Power cosmetic bag in Chapter 1 (page 22), this bag is "stitched" together using an ordinary stapler. The seams are then covered with duct tape to protect the staples and reinforce the "stitches." And you can embellish the tote with just about anything—pins, charms, or even a flowered ponytail holder like the one shown here. Bye-bye canvas book bag . . . hello style!

finished measurements
8" x 18¾" x 12" (20.5cm x 47.5cm x 30.5cm)

supplies
20" x 37" (51cm x 94cm) piece heavyweight fabric (such as canvas, patent leather vinyl, or oilcloth)

Masking tape

50" (127cm) of 1" (2.5cm) wide nylon webbing (for straps)

Stapler and staples

1½" wide duct tape (in contrasting color)

1. With right sides together, fold the fabric in half to create a 20" x 18½" (51cm x 47cm) rectangle, with the fold at the bottom.

2. Fold the top raw edges over to form a 2½" (6.5cm) "hem" on the top front and back. Use masking tape to temporarily hold the hems in place.

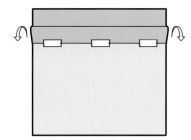

3. Cut the webbing in half to create two 25" (63.5 cm) straps. To attach each strap, mark a point 6" (15cm) in from each side of the bag. At

the marked point, staple one end of the strap with 4 or 5 staples, stapling through only the strap and the folded-over fabric so that the staples do not show on what will be the front of the bag. Repeat for the other end of the strap and then on the other side of the bag, making sure that the length and position of the straps match up.

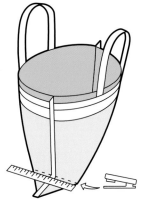

4. After the straps have been stapled into place, use 2 lengths of duct tape to cover the staples and to securely "hem" the top of the bag. Repeat on the other side.

6. Create the bottom: With the bag still inside out, flatten one corner to create a triangular point, aligning the side seam with the center bottom of the bag. Draw a 7½" (19cm) line perpendicular to the seam and 4" (10cm) from the corner point. Staple along the line. Repeat on the other side. Cover the staples with duct tape, if desired.

7. Turn the bag right side out. The fabric may feel stiff and hard to turn, but don't worry. Keep working at it, making sure to push out the bottom corners, and the bag will quickly take shape.

5. Sew up the sides: Staple each side of the bag using a ½" (13mm) seam allowance. Make sure the staples are very close together to create a straight, clean line. After you have stapled the sides, cover the staples with a long piece of duct tape (folded lengthwise over the raw edge).

i ♥ duct tape!

Where would we be without duct tape? First introduced during World War II as a protective sealant for ammunition cases, duct tape has become a staple in junk drawers and tool cupboards the world over. Now crafters are rolling out yards of the stuff and turning it into everything from purses to prom dresses.

duct tape: a brief chronological history

1940s Scientists at Permacell, a division of Johnson & Johnson, invent a tape to fill the need for a strong, durable, waterproof adhesive during World War II. The super-sticking tape was originally army green in color. Because it repelled water, it was nicknamed "duck tape."

1950s Put to civilian use holding metal air ducts together, the tape is changed to a silver color and becomes known as "duct tape."

1970 Crew members on *Apollo 13* use duct tape to assemble air scrubbers in space, saving the lives of the three astronauts on board.

1985 Duct tape is one of the main tools used by television action hero MacGyver, who can get himself out of almost any jam with this miraculous material.

2002 Doctors at the Madigan Army Medical Center in Tacoma, Washington, conduct a study showing that duct tape patches are extremely effective in removing warts.

2003 The U.S. Department of Homeland Security advises Americans to stock up on duct tape and plastic sheeting to protect themselves from a chemical or biological attack.

2004 The first official "Duct Tape Festival" is held in Avon, Ohio.

2007 Duck Brand duct tape introduces its twentieth color—aqua—joining such forerunners as flamingo, lime, and chrome.

it's a snap!

You can whip up this snappy little tote in less than an hour! It's made out of a large pillow cover with the zipper already sewn in (mine came from Ikea). Just fold up the bottom corners, position the straps, and snap them all into place. The tote packs up easily, so you can toss it in your purse to use for groceries or pack it in your suitcase for an extra travel bag.

finished measurements
9½" x 20" x 15½" (24cm x 51cm x 24cm)

supplies
20" (51cm) square zippered pillow cover with the zipper on a side seam
Iron and ironing board
48" (122cm) of 1" (2.5cm) wide nylon webbing (for straps)
Lighter or matches
6 colored snaps

1. Lay the pillow cover flat, right side out, with the zipper at the top. Fold up one of the bottom corners, aligning the corner point with the side seam and forming a triangle with the bottom edge that measures 9½" (24cm) across. (The distance from the point to the folded edge should be 4¾" [12cm].) Pin in place and iron. Repeat on the other side.

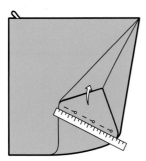

2. Secure the corners with snaps: Following the package instructions, attach a snap on one bottom corner of the bag—¾" (2cm) from the corner point—so that the corner can fold up and snap into place. Repeat on the other side.

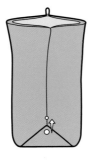

3. Prepare the straps: Cut the webbing in half to create two 24" (61cm) straps. Use a lighter or matches to "finish" the edges of the straps by quickly and carefully passing the flame back and forth over the ends. This will melt the edges and keep the straps from fraying. (Note: This works only with nylon or polypropylene webbing, *not* with cotton straps.)

4. Attach the straps: On one side of the bag, mark a point 6½" (16.5cm) in from each side and 1" (2.5cm) down from the top. Again following the package instructions, attach a bottom snap at each point. Then attach a top snap 1" (2.5cm) from each end of a strap. Snap the strap in place. Repeat on the back side of the bag to add the other strap.

pillow talk

Here's another take on turning a zippered pillow cover into a handy and handsome tote. The short, rolled straps and reinforced bottom make this bag a perfect choice for hauling heavier items. No longer a featherweight, this pillow cover tote goes the distance!

finished measurements
8" x 20" x 14" (20.5 x 51cm x 35.5cm)

supplies
Iron and ironing board
20" (51cm) square zippered pillow cover with the zipper on a side seam
Sewing machine
Thread
36" (91cm) of 1½" (3.8cm) wide cotton webbing (for straps)
Craft or "no-fray" glue
8" x 12" (20.5cm x 30.5cm) piece cardboard (or a legal-size, transparent plastic document envelope)
13" x 16" (33cm x 40.5cm) piece canvas

1. Iron the pillow cover so it's nice and flat.

2. Make the bottom: With the bag inside out and making sure the side and bottom seams line up, flatten the corners opposite the zipper to create triangular points. Draw a 7½" (19cm) line perpendicular to the side seam and 3½" (9cm) from the corner point. Sew across the line, backstitching at the beginning and end of the

seam to secure. Repeat on the other side. Turn the bag right side out.

3. Prepare the top: Push the zippered top in 1¾" (4.5cm), and pin in place. Iron flat, making sure the front and back line up.

4. Make the straps: Cut two 14" (35.5cm) straps from the webbing. Zigzag stitch back and forth over the cut edges on both straps to

keep the strap ends from fraying. Trim the threads. Lay one strap flat, and make a small mark 3" (7.5cm) from each end and ⅛" (3mm) from the side edge. Fold the strap in half lengthwise. Sewing close to the edge, stitch between the two marks (backstitching at the beginning and end of the seam) to create a folded handle. Place a thin line of glue over the zigzagged ends to finish them. Let dry. Repeat for the other strap.

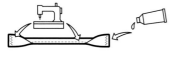

5. Make the false bottom (while waiting for the straps to dry): From the cardboard or document envelope, cut a piece smaller than the bag bottom (the piece should measure about 11½" x 7¼" [29cm x 18.5cm]). Fold the canvas piece in half with right sides together to make a 13" x 8" (33cm x 20.5cm) rectangle. Stitch down one long side and one end using a ½" (13mm) seam allowance. Clip the corners, and turn right side out. Iron flat. Slip the cardboard or plastic piece into the fabric sleeve you have just created.

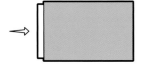

6. Turn the unfinished edge under ½" (13mm), and topstitch to close the edge. Place the covered piece in the bottom of the bag.

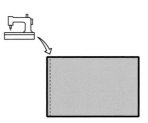

7. Attach the handles: Place the ends of one handle against the folded top edge, 6½" (16.5cm) in from each side of the bag. Pin to secure. On the front of the bag, sew a 1" x 1⅛" (2.5cm x 2.9cm) rectangle to attach one end of a

handle, sewing through the folded top edge *and* the strap. Reinforce by stitching diagonally from one corner to the other (as shown below). Be careful not to sew over the zipper. Repeat to join the other end of the handle. Attach the other handle to the back of the bag in the same manner.

storing your bags

Like a pair of nice shoes, your bags deserve the proper care when they're hanging out in your closet. Stuff your bags with white or natural-colored tissue paper to help hold their shape. Special occasion purses can be kept in a pillowcase or hatbox to keep them from fading and free of dust. Any bag that is made with tape should be stored in a cool place when it's not out on the town.

place mat tote

place mat tote

You'll have to look closely to see that this traditional-looking tote is actually made from a few woven place mats. Place mats make great bags! They're the perfect size to work with, and the finished edges make everything go much quicker. Doubled straps help reinforce the bag and make it quite sturdy. Not only are place mats easy to use—they're also readily available and inexpensive. The tote pictured here is fashioned from two striped place mats I picked up at Target for less than $3 each and a solid-colored mat I found at Pier One for under $5. At such prices, you can afford to make a tote for everyone seated at your table!

finished measurements

5½" x 17¾" x 14¼" (14cm x 45cm x 36cm)

supplies

4½ yd (4m) of 1" (2.5cm) wide cotton or nylon webbing (for straps)

Three 19" x 14" (48.5cm x 35.5cm) place mats (1 contrasting and 2 matching)

Sewing machine

Thread (to match webbing)

Stapler and staples (optional)

Duct tape (optional)

1. Make the "inside" straps: Cut 2 lengths of webbing, each 26" (66cm) long. Zigzag stitch back and forth over the raw ends to keep them from fraying.

2. Attach the inside straps to the two matching place mats: Lay out one place mat with the longer edge at the top. Measure 4½" (11.5cm) in from each side, and pin the straps to the inside top of the place mat, with the ends 1¼" (3cm) from the top edge. (There should be about 8" [20.5cm] between the straps.) Sew each end in place by stitching a small square over it. (The stitching will be covered by the outside strap, so don't worry if it isn't perfect!) Add a strap to the other matching place mat in the same way, making sure that the front and back straps line up.

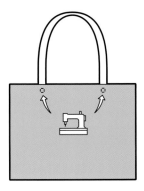

3. Attach the outside straps: Cut two more lengths of webbing, each 51" (129.5cm) long. (Note: You may need to cut these a little longer or shorter depending on

the size of your place mat.) Pin the outside strap over the inside strap and down the front of the bag, ending at the bottom of the place mat. Use a ruler to check that your straps are straight and an equal distance from the side edges. Topstitch the outside strap to the inside strap, beginning at the top of the place mat and sewing the strap handles together first. Then continue stitching down both sides on the front of the bag, sewing very close to the webbing edges. Repeat on the other matching place mat.

4. Attach the bottom of the bag: Pin the contrasting place mat to the *front* of the bag, overlapping the other place mat by 4" (10cm). Stitch the contrasting place mat to the bag front across the width

of the bag, topstitching close to the edge. Attach the bottom piece to the back of the bag in the same way.

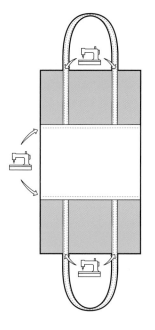

5. Sew up the side seams: Fold the joined piece in half, right sides together, matching top edge to top edge. Pin and sew each side using a ½" (13mm) seam allowance.

6. Make the bottom: With the bag still inside out, flatten one corner to create a triangular point, and draw a 5½" (14cm) line perpendicular to the seam and 2¾" (7cm) from the corner point. Sew along this line. (Note: If the fabric is too thick to go through your sewing machine, staple the seam instead. If you staple the seam, trim the fabric and cover the seam with duct tape to reinforce. Trim the tape along the seam to neaten the edge.) Repeat on the other side. Turn the bag right side out.

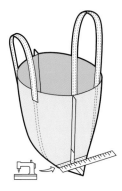

a note on needles

The needle you use can make a big difference in how your sewing machine sews. When working on heavier-weight materials, such as place mats or fabric shower curtains, try using a larger needle, such as a "90-14" or a "100-16" (the first number is the European number, followed by the smaller American number). If your stitches look jagged, you can try switching to a "sharp" needle, which will split the fabric fibers instead of going around them and will help keep your seams straight. But beware: "Sharps" will snag woven materials like T-shirts and knits, so use a "ball-point" needle on these kinds of fabrics. A good rule of thumb: Change your needle after every eight hours of sewing. Your machine and your stitches will thank you!

shower curtain tote

Who says your shower curtain has to stay in the shower? When I saw a stack of printed fabric shower curtains at a discount outlet, I couldn't snatch them up fast enough. They were so inexpensive—the same amount of material at a fabric store would have cost three times as much! The panels were made from heavyweight canvas, just the right weight for a casual tote or purse. And the best part: The metal grommets at the top were perfectly positioned to hold the bag's straps. Check out discount stores, eBay, and the sale sections of home catalogs for bargain finds. You'll never look at a shower curtain the same way again.

finished measurements
7" x 20½" x 14" (18cm x 52cm x 35.5cm)

supplies
Fabric shower curtain with metal grommets (100% cotton works best)

Shower Curtain Tote pattern template (page 120)

Sewing machine

Thread (to match shower curtain)

Iron and ironing board

1. Cut out the bag pieces: Center the Shower Curtain Tote pattern template (page 120) on the fabric. Line up the top edge of the template with the finished top of the shower curtain, and center the template on a grommet (the bag will have 3 grommets across the top). Cut out the front of the bag. Repeat to cut out the back of the bag. (Note: If the pattern on your shower curtain isn't complicated, you can cut the front and back together. Just double the fabric, lining up the grommets.) Save the leftover fabric for the straps.

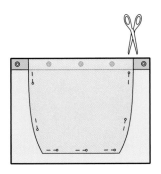

2. Make the darts: On the wrong side of one cut fabric piece, fold the bottom left corner (as shown above right). Mark a point 4¾" (12cm) up the fold from the corner. Mark another point 3" (7.5cm)

along the raw bottom. Connect the points to create the dart line. Repeat on the right bottom corner and then on both bottom corners of the other cut fabric piece.

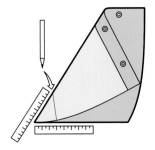

3. Sew each dart by stitching on the drawn line. Press the darts toward the center. Trim the seam allowances on the darts to ⅝" (1.5cm). Zigzag stitch the raw edges to keep them from fraying.

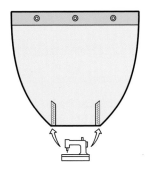

4. Pin the bag pieces with right sides together, and sew around the raw edges using a ½" (13mm) seam allowance. Zigzag stitch the raw edges together to keep them from fraying. Turn the bag right side out.

5. Add the straps: From the leftover fabric, cut a 2" x 71" (5cm x 180cm) strip. On one of the short ends, fold the fabric in half so the right sides are together. Stitch 1" (2.5cm) across using a ½" (13mm) seam allowance. Clip the corner. Turn the fabric right side out, fold the long strip of fabric in half widthwise, and iron. Turn under ½" (13mm) along the open edges to create a 1" x 70" (2.5cm x 178cm) strap. Press the hem in place. Topstitch ⅛" (3mm) from the edge on all four sides to finish. Thread the strap through the side grommets and knot the ends on the inside, adjusting the straps to your liking.

3

bag lady
purses and handbags

Purses and handbags are at the top of the fashion food chain these days. In fact, the bag a woman carries has become much more than a useful accessory—it has morphed into the ultimate fashion statement, a status symbol, and a general object of desire. So, in a day and age when handbags can cost more than a month's salary, there's something quite appealing about leaving the designer purses on their fancy shelves and making your own unique bags instead.

The purses in this chapter are made from easy-to-find, inexpensive materials. But if you do happen to come across some luscious wool or sumptuous upholstery fabric, don't be afraid to use it! And even though you're supplementing your bag wardrobe with some homemade goodies, you can still lust after that Kelly bag you've always wanted. Or, you can flip to page 61 and make your own designer bag out of a T-shirt and duct tape! Either way, you'll carry it off.

keyhole clutch

This is one of my favorite little purses. The shape of this bag is so versatile and, depending on the fabric you use, the bag can be either elegant or sporty. The secret is to line the fabric with strips of duct tape so that the finished purse holds it shape. Then just toss your keys and cell phone inside, and you're ready to go!

finished measurements
3½" x 14¾" x 7¾" (9cm x 37.5cm x 19.5cm)

supplies
16" x 21" (40.5cm x 53.5cm) piece heavyweight fabric, such as printed canvas, linen, denim, or upholstery fabric
Lint roller (optional)
Duct tape (in complementary color)
Stapler and staples
Iron and ironing board

1. Fold the fabric in half to create a 16" x 10½" (40.5cm x 26.5cm) rectangle, with the fold at the bottom. Cut out corner notches, 1¾" (4.5cm) wide and 1¼" (3cm) high, on the bottom folded edge (as shown below).

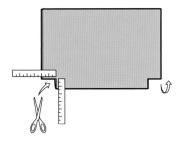

2. Open the fabric, wrong side up, on a flat, hard surface. Remove any bits of fuzz or thread before you start duct taping the fabric (you may want to use a lint roller for this step). Once the fabric is smooth and clean, cover it with strips of duct tape, placed horizontally and overlapping slightly, until the entire piece has been lined.

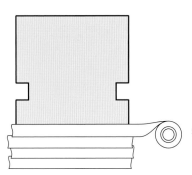

3. Trim the tape around the fabric outline to neaten the edges.

4. Make the handles: With right sides together, fold the fabric in half so that the corner notches are again at the bottom. Mark a point at the center of the bag width and 1¾" (4.5cm) down from the top edge. Draw a 4" x 1" (10cm x 2.5cm) rectangle, using the mark as the top center point. (This will be the cutout for the handle.)

5. Before cutting, draw a line dividing the rectangle in half

9. Clip the corners at the top of the bag. Place the bag, side seam up, over the arm of your ironing board. Use your fingers or an unplugged, cold iron to press the seam open. Cover the flattened seam with duct tape. Repeat on the other side.

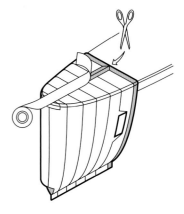

horizontally. Then mark two points on the drawn line, ¾" (2cm) in from each side. Draw a line from each corner to the nearest marked point on the center line to make cutting lines.

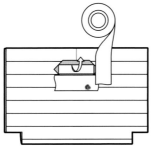

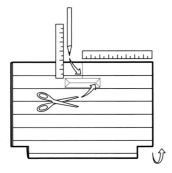

6. Cut on the diagonal lines to form triangular side flaps. Then cut down the remaining center line to form top and bottom flaps. Fold back all four flaps, and tape them down with duct tape to form the keyhole handle. Make a keyhole handle on the back of the bag in the same manner.

7. Fold the top edge of the bag over ¾" (2cm), and secure it with a strip of duct tape, trimming the tape around the handle opening. Repeat on the back of the bag.

8. With right sides together, staple the sides of the bag using a ½" (13mm) seam allowance.

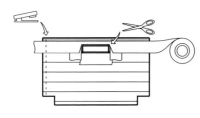

10. Make the bottom: Close the bottom of the bag at the corners by matching up the raw edges. Staple closed using a ½" (13mm) seam allowance. Cover the edges with duct tape (folded lengthwise over the raw edge), and trim. Repeat on the other side. Turn the bag right side out.

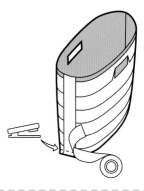

place mat purse

place mat purse

Looking for something to do with that lone place mat you have in the cupboard or that sample mat you found marked down at your favorite housewares store? Well, you can always set a lovely table for one—*or* you can make a little purse! Just add a colorful flower and bamboo handles (available at ribbon and trimming stores or online; see Resources, page 116), and you'll be ready to head out for lunch, bag in hand.

finished measurements

2½" x 10" x 8¼" (6.5cm x 25.5cm x 21cm)

supplies

19" x 13" (48.5cm x 33cm) woven place mat

Masking tape

Sewing machine

Heavy-duty sewing machine needle, such as a 90-14 or 100-16

Thread (to match place mat)

21" x 13" (53.5cm x 33cm) piece heavy lining material, such as canvas

Iron and ironing board

Fabric or silk flower

Sharp pencil or wooden skewer

Scrap of duct tape

1 yd (91.5cm) of ⅝" (1.5cm) wide grosgrain ribbon (in complementary color)

Two 5½" (14 cm) wide bamboo purse handles, with bottom hardware already attached

4 small Velcro self-sticking dots

1. With right sides together, fold the place mat in half, matching the short edges with the fold at the bottom. Use strips of masking tape to temporarily hold the sides together.

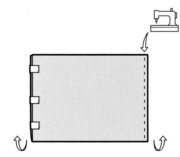

2. Sew the sides together using a ¼" (6mm) seam allowance, removing the masking tape as you go. (Note: If your place mat is really thick, you may need to help feed the fabric manually.) Backstitch back and forth at the beginning and end of the seams to reinforce.

3. Make the bottom: With the purse still inside out, fold the bottom corner to form a triangular point. Draw a 2" (5cm) line perpendicular to the side seam and 1½" (3.8cm) from the corner point. Sew along the line. Backstitch back and forth at the beginning and end of the seam to reinforce.

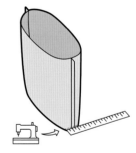

4. Carefully turn the bag right side out.

5. Make the lining: Zigzag stitch the short sides of the lining material to keep the edges from fraying.

Next, fold the material in half, right sides together, to create a 13" x 10½" (33cm x 26.5cm) rectangle, with the fold at the bottom. Pin the sides together, and sew them using a ⅜" (1cm) seam allowance. (This will make the lining slightly smaller than the purse so that it can fit neatly inside.) Finish the bottom of the lining in the same manner as the purse, creating triangular points 2" (5cm) wide and 1½" (3.8cm) from the corner point. With the lining still inside out, fold the top edge down 1¼" (3cm) toward the outside and press. Drop the lining, wrong side out, into the bag to see whether it fits. You may need to fold the top down a little more or less, depending on the size of your place mat.

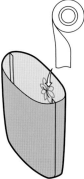

6. Add the flower: Temporarily remove the lining from the bag. Remove the green plastic "calyx"—the little base at the bottom—from the back of the artificial flower, leaving the stem in place. Center the flower on the top front of the bag, and mark the spot where the stem hits. Use a sharp pencil or wooden skewer to poke a hole for the stem. Place the flower through the hole, and carefully slit the stem in half so that it can be flattened out on the inside of the bag. Secure the flower with 2 pieces of duct tape crossed over the flattened stem.

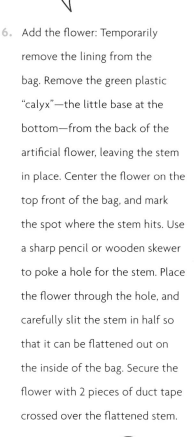

7. Add the handles: Cut four 6" (15cm) pieces of grosgrain ribbon. Fold each ribbon in half, and stitch the short ends together using a ½" (13mm) seam allowance. Turn the ribbon loops inside out to hide the seam. Iron flat. Fold

the ribbon loops over the handle rings, and pin them in place. Using a ¼" (6mm) seam allowance, sew the ribbon loops to the handles first (before you sew the handles to the bag). Then center the first handle on the front of the bag, and pin the ribbon loops in place on the inside of the bag. Stitch the loops to the place mat, sewing on the *inside* of the bag, stitching back and forth a few times to reinforce. Attach the remaining handle to the back of the bag in the same manner. Trim all seams.

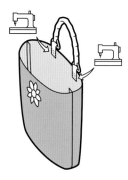

8. Add the lining: Drop the lining back into the bag. Following the package instructions, attach the lining to the bag using Velcro self-sticking dots.

pillow cover hobo bag

finished measurements
18" x 12¾" (45.5cm x 32.5cm)

supplies
18" (45.5cm) square zippered pillow cover
Pillow Cover Hobo Bag pattern template (page 121)
Sewing machine
Thread
Iron and ironing board

Turn a pretty floral pillow cover into a curvy hobo bag in just a few steps. The one pictured here is made from an 18" (45.5cm) square cover with the zipper already sewn in. If you use a larger or smaller pillow cover, adjust the size of the pattern template on a copy machine, making sure the side edges of the pattern line up with the side edges of the pillow.

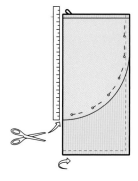

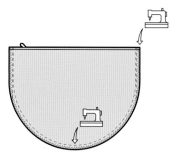

1. Cut out the bag: Turn the pillow cover inside out, and close the zipper halfway. Fold the pillow cover in half, matching side edge to side edge, with the zipper at the top. Place the straight edge of the Hobo Bag pattern template (page 121) on the center fold and the top of the pattern up next to the zipper. Pin the pattern in place; then cut. Save the leftover fabric for the strap. (Note: Depending on where the pillow cover's zipper is located, you may need to adjust the position of your template before cutting. Just make sure that the bottom of your pattern hits 13½" [34.5cm] from the zipper seam.)

2. Sew the bag: Unfold the bag. With the bag still inside out, pin the raw edges together. Starting at one top edge, stitch around the curved edge using a ½" (13mm) seam allowance. (Note: You will be stitching over existing seams at the top of the bag.) Zigzag stitch the raw edges of the seam allowance together to keep the fabric from fraying. Turn the bag right side out. Press and set it aside.

3. Cut out the strap: Use the fabric left from the bottom of the pillow cover. With right sides facing out, and with the pillow's bottom and side seams still in place, cut out a 3½" x 18" (9cm x 45.5cm) rectangle, aligning one of the long edges with the bottom fold. Leave the seam at the bottom of the bag in place, but trim off the sewn seams on both 4" (10cm) sides, so that the ends are open.

4. Sew the strap: Turn the strap fabric so that the *wrong* sides are together. Turn the open, long edge under ½" (13mm) on the front and back. Press in place. Topstitch this side of the strap closed using a ⅛" (3mm) seam allowance. Top-stitch on the other long side of the strap (which is already closed) to match.

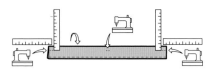

5. Make the strap pleats: Fold the strap in half lengthwise, matching the long edges, and gently press with your iron. Starting ⅝" (1.5cm) away from the fold at one short end of the strap, sew a ½" (13mm) long seam parallel to the fold. Pleat the opposite end of the strap in the same manner.

   To make a pleat in the center of the strap, first find and mark the midpoint of the strap (mea-suring end to end). At the center point, sew a short ½" (13mm) seam parallel to the fold (just as you did at each end).

6. Unfold the fabric, and press the pleat flat along the entire length of the strap. Machine-baste the pleats in place parallel and close to the strap end. Repeat on the other end.

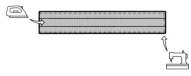

7. Attach the strap: With the bag right side out, push in the top corners near the zipper to form pockets for the strap ends. Pin the corners so that the outside edge measures about 2¾" (7cm) across. Press. (Note: The folded pocket edge should be at least ½" [13mm] from the end of the zipper.)

8. On the inside of the bag, cut off a small portion of the corner, 1" (2.5cm) from the end of the zip-per, to create an opening so that the strap can fit neatly in place. Repeat on the other side.

9. Pin the strap ends in place, and then hand-baste them in place on the inside of the bag. (Don't worry about how your hand-basting looks; it will be removed later.)

10. With the strap basted in place, draw a seam line ⅝" (1.5cm) from the line you cut in step 7. Machine-stitch on the line, backstitching at the beginning and end to secure. (Note: You may need to help feed your fabric through by turning the wheel of your machine by hand.) Attach the opposite strap end to the other side in the same manner. Remove the hand-basting, and turn the bag right side out.

tee-time

tee-time

This bag should really be called a Zoe bag since it was my friend's daughter, Zoe, who inspired the design. When I told her I wanted to make some bags out of T-shirts, she suggested I come up with an over-the-shoulder style and shared her favorite places to get cheap tees. With Zoe in mind, I started thinking about how to put a new twist on an old T-shirt. I was folding up some ordinary plastic shopping bags when it hit me! As I flattened the plastic bag out, I realized that it looked like a sleeveless tank top. I started playing around with the shape, eventually turning the bag on its side so that the handles made a cute arched strap. Redoing the bottom while the bag was oriented on its side added the finishing touch. Like the Keyhole Clutch (page 52), this bag is lined with duct tape to give it structure.

You can make this bag from any size of T-shirt: Kid's sizes turn into handheld purses, and men's shirts make large totes. The one pictured here was made from a size large woman's T-shirt. No matter what size you use, this bag will suit you to a T!

finished measurements
5¾" x 15¾" x 20" (14.5cm x 40cm x 51cm) including the strap

supplies
T-shirt (the larger the shirt, the larger the bag)
Iron and ironing board
4 rolls 1½" wide duct tape (or 1 roll 2" wide duct tape)
Pencil
Stapler and staples

1. Lay the T-shirt out flat. Cut off the sleeves, trimming as close to the seam as possible. Leave the neck in place for the moment.

2. Turn the shirt inside out, and iron out the wrinkles. Line the shirt with vertical strips of duct tape, overlapping the edges slightly and smoothing any wrinkles as best you can. (It may help to rotate the shirt around the arm of your ironing board when taping the sides.) Trim the duct tape edges around the collar, armholes, and bottom as you go to keep the tape from sticking to everything.

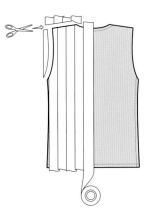

3. Turn the shirt right side out, and lay it flat. Fold the shirt in half lengthwise, matching the shoulder seams, side seams, and bottom edges.

4. Using a pencil, draw the straps and side (as shown). With the shirt still folded, carefully cut just inside the pencil marks as cleanly as possible. Open the shirt up—it will look like a tank top.

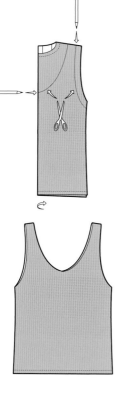

5. Turn the shirt sideways, and fold it so that the side seams line up and become the middle of the bag. The "tank top" straps are now the

handles. Trim more fabric, if narrower straps are desired.

6. Make the bottom: Turn the bag inside out. Draw a straight line across the bottom of the bag, making sure to draw above the shirt's hem. Staple along this line, and trim the edges to ½" (13mm).

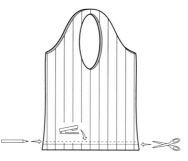

Cover the seam with duct tape (folded lengthwise over the raw edge).

Fold the corners to form a triangular point. Draw a 6" (15cm) line 2¾" (7cm) above the point. Staple along the line. Trim the edges to ½" (13mm), and duct tape the seams. Repeat on the other corner.

7. Turn the bag right side out.

shower power

This casual bag is another shower curtain creation. I wanted to keep it as simple as possible and find a way to line the bag without undoing the shower curtain's finished edge and grommets. The answer came in a roll of iron-on vinyl. I originally bought this fusible laminate to use with cosmetic bags because it's waterproof and it protects the attached fabric. But then I realized that I could also use it to add heft to the shower curtain material. Once you start experimenting with this iron-on vinyl, you won't want to stop. You could even line some ordinary fabric or a bed sheet and turn that into a shower curtain. Now there's a twist!

finished measurements
6" x 14½" x 9" (15cm x 37cm x 23cm)

supplies
Fabric shower curtain with metal grommets (100% cotton works best)
1 package 17" x 2 yd (43cm x 1.8m) iron-on vinyl (see Resources, page 116, for more info)
Lint roller
Iron and ironing board
Sewing machine
Thread
1¼ yd (114.5cm) of 1" (2.5cm) wide nylon webbing (for straps)
Lighter or matches
4 self-closing "lobster-claw" hooks (available at hardware stores)

1. Cut out the fabric: Cut two 16" x 12" (40.5cm x 30.5cm) pieces of fabric from the shower curtain, centering 2 grommets across the top (as shown).

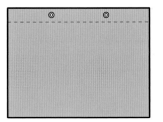

2. Cut out and apply the vinyl: Cut two 16" x 10½" (40.5cm x 26.5cm) pieces of iron-on vinyl to cover the wrong side of the fabric pieces, starting below the hemmed top edge. Use a lint roller to remove all lint and threads from the fabric surface. Apply the vinyl following the package instructions.

3. Sew the darts: With one of the fabric pieces wrong side up, fold one bottom corner by lining up the side edge with the bottom edge. Mark a point 2½" (6.5cm) along the bottom edge. Mark a second point 5" (12.5cm) up the fold. Connect the two points to draw the dart. Pin the fabric together, and stitch along the drawn line. Repeat on the opposite corner. Make the two darts on the second fabric piece in the same manner.

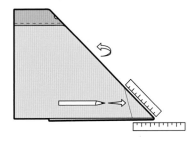

4. Flatten the darts, pressing them toward the center of the fabric piece. Trim the bottom edge of each dart to align with the bottom edge of the fabric.

5. Form the bag: With the right sides together, pin the front piece to the back piece, making sure the darts are folded toward the center. Sew the side and bottom edges together using a ½" (13mm) seam allowance.

lint hint

Keep a lint roller on hand to help you pick up unwanted scraps, threads, pins, and, of course, lint! Not only will a lint roller help free your fabric of stray threads and fuzz, but this inexpensive tool will also work wonders around your sewing machine and cutting table, especially if your assembly area is carpeted. There's no need to drag out your vacuum and risk jamming it up with pins or stray staples— the sticky lint tape makes cleaning up a piece of cake. (And yes, it even works on crumbs!)

6. Clip the top corners on the diagonal in the seam allowance. Clean up the bag edges by trimming around the bag, cutting off any loose threads. Zigzag stitch the seams together to finish the edges. Trim the threads, and turn the bag right side out.

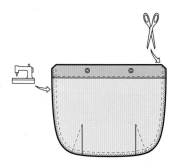

7. Make the straps: Cut two 18½" (47cm) pieces from the nylon webbing. Use a lighter or matches to "finish" the strap ends by quickly and carefully passing the flame back and forth over the ends. This will melt the edges and keep the straps from fraying. (Note: This works only with nylon or polypropylene webbing, *not* with cotton straps.)

8. Thread each strap end through a hook. Turn the end under 1¾" (4.5cm) and pin to enclose the hook. (The finished strap should measure 15" (38cm) long, not including the hooks.) Stitch the doubled end of the strap twice to secure. Repeat for the other strap. Attach the hooks to the bag through the grommets.

extreme makeover: purse edition

Rescue an old bag from a thrift store, tag sale, or online auction, and give it a new look. A beautiful handle or closer found on a ripped or worn purse can be repurposed and used on a new bag. Or simply cover an old bag with new fabric for a purse that is truly one of a kind.

online thrift stores

The auction site eBay is always a good place to start when hunting online. But I've also found some treasures on the sites below:

www.shopgoodwill.com

www.housingworksauctions.com

www.craigslist.org

fancy that!

evening bags and small purses

An evening bag, like a beautiful piece of jewelry, can "make" an outfit. But scrambling at the last minute to find just the right bag for an evening out can feel anything but elegant. Instead of panicking on a Saturday night about where you're going to stash your lipstick and keys, throw together one of the pretty little bags in this chapter on Saturday afternoon, and you'll be ready for any outing. Many of the purses included here are so easy that it will literally take you less time to make your own bag than it would to go out and buy one. And they're so much fun to whip up!

Since evening bags don't have to withstand the constant abuse of an everyday purse, you can experiment with more unusual materials. The Climbing the Walls bag (page 83), for example, is made from a beautiful piece of wallpaper. Another (Nights in Black Satin, page 70) is made from satin ribbon with a rhinestone earring clasp. Like the make-up bags in the first chapter, these bags take very little material—experiment with a variety of colors and fabrics. Not only will you have just the right bag for that special occasion, you'll also be toting an original. Now what's more elegant than that?

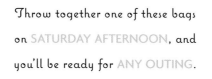

Throw together one of these bags on SATURDAY AFTERNOON, and you'll be ready for ANY OUTING.

nights in black satin

This bag is constructed very much like the Caution! bag in Chapter 1 (page 31), only this time the fabric is made from layered silk ribbon instead of "CAUTION" tape (or try it with grosgrain ribbon for a less formal version). The heavyweight, gold-coated zipper—placed just under the flap—lends a dressiness to the bag. A stray rhinestone earring doubles as a faux clasp, but you could also use an ornate pearl pin, a vintage button, or even a chandelier crystal. After all, anything and everything goes with black satin!

finished measurements

9½" x 5¾" (24cm x 12cm), closed

9½" x 9½" (24cm x 24 cm), open

supplies

2½ yd (228.5cm) of 3" (7.5cm) wide satin ribbon

Duct tape (in matching color)

20" (51cm) long heavyweight coat zipper

Scotch matte-finish "Magic" tape

Stapler and staples

Masking tape

Clip earring, button, pin, or crystal (for faux clasp)

1. Make the "fabric": Cut seven 12" (30.5cm) strips of satin ribbon. Begin with 1 ribbon strip, *shiny side down*. Cover the ribbon with a strip of duct tape, sticky side down. Place a second strip of duct tape, sticky side down, so that it overlaps the edge of the first tape strip. Turn the swatch over. Lay down a second ribbon strip so that it slightly overlaps the first ribbon and sticks to the exposed tape. Continue laying down ribbons and tape in this manner, overlapping them slightly and flipping the fabric over and back as you go, until all 7 strips of ribbon are connected.

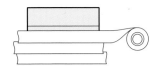

2. Trim the sides of the ribbon-tape swatch to create an 11" (28cm) wide piece of fabric. One short end will be the top of the bag.

3. Attach the zipper: Place the zipper face down, aligned with the top edge of the fabric.

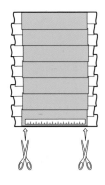

(The slider end of the zipper should be ¾" [2cm] from the side edge.) Use Scotch "Magic" tape to temporarily hold the zipper in place.

4. Staple one side of the zipper in place, placing the staples ¼" (6mm) from the top edge (you may need to open the zipper to keep the zipper tape flat and the seam straight).

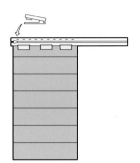

5. Remove the Scotch "Magic" tape. Turn the fabric over, flatten out the zipper, and cover the staples with a strip of duct tape. Trim any excess duct tape, leaving the extra zipper length for the moment.

6. Fold the bag in half, right sides together, aligning the other side of the zipper with the back top raw edge. Use masking tape to temporarily hold the bag sides together.

7. Staple the loose side of the zipper to the other top edge (opening the zipper as needed to keep the staples straight). Remove the masking tape. As with the other side, flatten out the zipper and cover the staples with a strip of duct tape. Trim any excess duct tape, but keep the extra zipper length intact for the moment.

8. With the bag still inside out and the zipper closed, flatten the bag so that the zipper pull is on the *right-hand* side and the zipper teeth are about 4¾" (12cm) from the bottom of the bag and 5¼" (13.5cm) from the top. (The zipper needs to fall on the bottom half of the bag so that when the bag is folded to form the clutch, the zipper is just slightly below the fold.) Crease the edges, and use masking tape to temporarily hold the sides together.

9. Staple the sides together using a ½" (13mm) seam allowance, removing the masking tape as you go and *opening the zipper* before you staple over it. Staple over the zipper as best you can.

10. Trim the extra zipper length. Fold duct tape over the raw edge of the side seams.

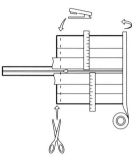

11. Carefully turn the bag inside out, gently pushing out the corners. Fold the top over, covering the zipper and creating a "flap."

12. Clip the earring to the front of the flap, centering it on the bottom edge. Mark where the clip falls on the back of the flap. Use a seam ripper to make a slit between the pencil mark and the edge of the bag (on the back of the flap only) so that the earring clip can slide through. Clip the earring through the slit. Cover the back of the clip with duct tape.

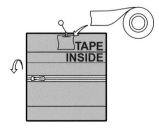

barneys bag

barneys bag

I love browsing through specialty stores and boutiques for ideas and, if I'm lucky, the occasional marked-down gem. On one of my window-shopping sojourns to Barneys on Madison Avenue, I found a scrumptious silk place mat in the home section. Unfortunately, it was not in the bargain bin! In other words, setting a whole table with these would have been prohibitive (not to mention a real disaster if someone spilled red wine on them). But I decided to splurge on a lone specimen, to see what I could make out of it.

My place mat was lined with equally beautiful fabric, so turning it into an evening bag took only about fifteen minutes! When looking for a place mat for this bag, choose one made from two pieces of fabric sewn together. This will allow you to easily sew a casing for the handles at the top and will provide an instant lining for the bag. No one has to know that your Barneys Bag actually started out as a place mat. Bon appétit!

finished measurements

11" x 7" (28cm x 18cm)

supplies

14" x 16" (35.5cm x 40.5cm) fancy place mat (made from two pieces of fabric sewn together)

Sewing machine

Thread (in matching color)

Seam ripper

Two 6" (15cm) wide bamboo handles, with metal base rod

1. Fold the place mat in half (right sides together), with the fold at the bottom, to create a 14" x 8" (35.5cm x 20.5cm) rectangle. Pin the sides together. Sew the side seams using a scant ¼" (6mm) seam allowance, stopping 2½" (6.5cm) from the top edge on each side and backstitching at the beginning and end to secure.

2. Turn the bag right side out. Use a seam ripper to carefully open the top side edge seam, starting ½" (13mm) from the top and ripping out only a few stitches, so that the metal handle rod can slip through it. Repeat on the three other top side edges.

3. Sew a "casing" for the handle rod by stitching a seam on the top edge of the bag using a ⅝" (1.5cm) seam allowance and backstitching a few stitches at the beginning and end of the seam to secure. Repeat on the other top edge.

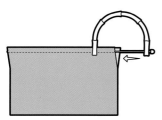

4. Slip the metal rod of the handle through the handle and casing. Screw the rod into place. Repeat with the other handle. Adjust the bottom corners of the bag to get the shape you want.

5. Pour yourself that glass of red wine, and enjoy!

mini bags

Don't throw out those fabric scraps—use them to make mini bags! Minis take practically no material at all and can be turned into magnets, used as ornaments, attached as gift tags, or fancied into key chains. But beware, minis are often "snatched" and relocated to dollhouses and children's jewelry boxes. The solution, of course, is to just make more!

bag jewelry

Adorn your bag by attaching an eye-catching charm to a silk ribbon and tying it around one handle. Use a brass washer from the hardware store, a stray engraved charm or medallion (found at flea markets), or a decorative bead. Your bag will love its new bangle.

the envelope, please

This bag was inspired by an article in the Style section of the *New York Times*. The story featured photos of metallic "dazzler" bags, including purses made by Louis Vuitton and a silver Chanel handbag with adjustable straps. These beautiful bags, made with top-end materials, resembled quilted Mylar balloons! Although it took some improvising, and a long list of supplies, this "Chanel bag" made out of a silver bubble mailing envelope actually turned out to be pretty easy. I added grommets and used a nickel-plated dog leash for the chain. While an authentic metallic Chanel bag retails for about $2,100, this one cost less than $15 to make! And don't you think it would look dazzling (and maybe even fool a few folks) on the red carpet?

finished measurements
4" x 9½" x 5½" (10cm x 24cm x 14cm)

supplies
10½" x 13½" (26.5cm x 34.5cm) silver bubble mailing envelope, with flap on the wide side (see Resources, page 116)

Masking tape

Black permanent marker, such as a Sharpie

Silver (not gray) duct tape or clear packing tape

2 large colored, vinyl-coated paper clips

Stapler and staples

1" (2.5cm) wide Velcro self-sticking tape

Four ⅜" (9mm) silver grommets

Grommet tool (or grommet pliers)

48" (122cm) medium-weight (2.5mm chain links) nickel-plated chain dog leash (ask the hardware store to clip off the leash handle and hook, which you can save for another project)

⅝" (1.5cm) diameter metal key ring

Hot glue gun and glue sticks

Two-piece zinc-plated hardware, such as a bracket, mending brace, or latch (to form the faux clasp)

1. Make the body of the bag: Open the bubble envelope, and flatten out one bottom corner to create a triangular point, aligning the side seam with the center bottom of the bag. The folded edge should measure about 3½" (9cm) across and about 2" (5cm) from the end point. Push the corner *inside* the bag to form the bottom. Use masking tape inside to temporarily hold the corner in place (it will be stapled on the inside later). Repeat on the other side.

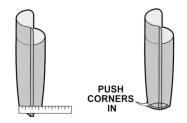

PUSH CORNERS IN

2. With the flap standing up on the left, and using the marker, mark a point 6¼" (16cm) up the side seams. From this mark, draw a 1" (2.5cm) perpendicular line toward the back of the bag, and mark the end of the line with a point. On the very top of the envelope, on the flap, measure 1" (2.5cm) from the seam and mark with another point. Connect the two points with a straight line. (You will have drawn what looks like a large "L.")

(The bag body, not including the flap, should now measure about 5½" [14cm] tall.)

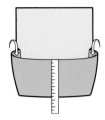

5. On the *inside* of the bag, place 1" wide strips of duct tape (made by tearing a 2" wide strip down the middle [see box on page 13 for more on duct tape measurments]) to tape down the folded over sides near the inside back edges and the folded over front edge.

6. Finish the front flap: Use 1" wide strips of duct tape to "hem" the front flap edges, folding them over ½" (13mm) on the sides and 1" (2.5cm) on the top. Fold the side edges first, then the top, making the corners as neat as possible. If your envelope came with a Velcro closure, remove the Velcro piece from the front flap before you "hem" the top edge. (Tear it off as best as you can. Don't worry if this damages a little of the inside bubble wrap; just make sure not to tear through to the front.)

Next draw a diagonal line from the bottom corner of the "L" down ½" (13mm) and over ½" (13mm) (as shown). Repeat on the other side, noting that the "L" on the other side will look reversed.

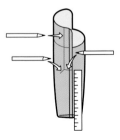

3. Cut on the long vertical line and short diagonal *only*; leave the

horizontal line intact. Trim away the extra top flap so that the remaining flap is even with the front raw edge. Repeat on the other side.

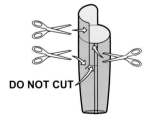

DO NOT CUT

4. Fold the raw side and front edges 2½" (6.5cm) to the inside of the bag to form a finished edge.

7. Pleat the side seams: Fold in the side seams to form a 1¼" (3cm) pleat so that the front flap lays nicely over the body of the bag. Use a paper clip to temporarily hold the pleats in place.

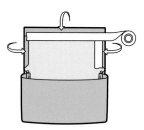

8. Open and close the bag, making sure it looks the way you want. If need be, adjust the pleats and push or pull out the bottom corners (remove the masking tape first) to get exactly the shape you want. Once you're happy with how the bag looks, remove the paper clips and draw a line on the inside of the bag with a fine-point marker to show where the bottom seams should be. Staple the seam on the inside of the bag, pulling the corners in a bit so you can staple on the line. Repeat on the other side.

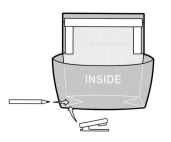

9. Cover the inside bottom with 2 strips of 2" wide duct tape to keep the corners flat and to cover the staples.

10. Add the new Velcro closure: Cut a 2" (5cm) piece of Velcro self-sticking tape, and tape the opposing pieces to the center of the front flap and main bag, aligned with each other.

11. Put in the grommets: Place a set of grommets 1" (2.5cm) in from the edge on the top of the flap (use a grommet tool for best results). Insert a second set of grommets on the back of the bag, just behind and below the first set. (You may need to angle the grommets closer to the bag edge to use

the grommet tool, because it can't reach very far from the edge.)

12. Lace the dog leash chain through all four grommets to create two adjustable straps. Connect the ends of the chain on the inside using a small key ring.

13. Using a glue gun, make your own decorative clasp from the hardware pieces. Glue the finished "clasp" to the front flap.

channeling chanel

When Coco Chanel introduced her quilted bag with a chain shoulder strap in February 1955, she took the fashion world by storm. She said she found her inspiration for the quilted design from the jackets that riders wore at the racetrack. Chanel added eyelets to the bag, threaded a leather-laced chain strap through them, and the classic Chanel bag was born. The bag was named the "2.55 bag," shorthand for the month and year it was created. Since then, it has been made in almost every color and material imaginable and has remained the ultimate "it" bag.

fringe benefits

Katherine, a fourth grader who came to the Craft Corner I ran at my children's school, was a very enthusiastic crafter and was simply mad for fringe. She fringed everything we made. Belts, picture frames, bookmarks—whatever it was, she found a way to add some feathery trim! Her fringe obsession inspired me to start snipping away at strips of my beloved duct tape. The resulting fringe looked a bit like textured patent leather, and I discovered that by using two different widths of tape, the strips became "self-sticking"! The chain straps on this bag—a nod to Coco Chanel—are attached with inexpensive "S" hooks. This purse is completely no-sew and is so much fun to make! Every time I use it, it reminds me that you never know who or what will inspire you—and that creativity is contagious.

finished measurements
9" x 9" (23cm x 23cm)

supplies
2" wide duct tape
Stapler and staples
1½" wide duct tape (in color to match 2" wide duct tape)
Four ⅜" (9mm) diameter brass grommets
Grommet tool (or grommet pliers)
Four 1" (2.5cm) brass open "S" hooks
Two 12" (30.5cm) pieces of #2 brass chain (links approximately ⅞" [2.2cm]) (available at hardware stores)
Pliers

1. Make a piece of duct tape fabric: Using 2" wide duct tape, place a 12" (30.5cm) strip of tape on the work surface, sticky side up. Cut a second strip of tape, and place it, sticky side up, so that it slightly overlaps the first piece. Then place another strip, sticky side *down*, across the seam of the first two pieces. Continue layering the tape on the front and back, overlapping the tape slightly and flip-ping the fabric over as needed to attach the strips to one another. When the piece has reached just over 20" (51cm) long, fold the edges of the tape over at the top and bottom to "finish" them. Trim the sides to create a 9" x 20" (23cm x 51cm) piece of fabric.

2. Fold the fabric piece in half, with the fold at the bottom, to form a 9" x 10" (23cm x 25.5cm) rectangle. At the fold, pinch up 1" (2.5cm) to form a pleat at the bottom (this will help form the bag bottom). The bag should now measure 9" (23cm) tall.

3. Taper the bag sides: With the pleat still at the bottom, cut a

diagonal taper along the sides so that the bag measures 8" (20.5cm) across the top and 9" (23cm) across the bottom.

4. Staple the pleat on each side of the bag bottom using a couple of staples near the edge.

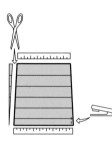

5. Tape the side seams with a strip of 2" [5cm] wide duct tape (folded lengthwise over the raw edge and folded over toward the inside on the top edge). Trim the excess tape at the bottom.

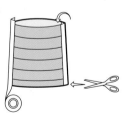

6. Make the fringe: Cut a 20" (51cm) strip of duct tape from each width of tape (2" and 1½"). Lay the 1½" wide strip over the 2" wide strip, placing sticky sides together and lining up the bot-

tom edges. Make a total of 6 strips in this manner, and "fringe" 5 of them by clipping strips approximately ⅛" (3mm) wide and 1¼" (3cm) long with scissors.

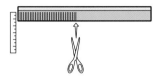

7. Take a break, make a cup of tea, and let your hands rest from all that fringing!

8. Attach the fringe: Draw a line across the bag about 2" (5cm) from the bottom edge. Place your first fringed strip even with this line, wrapping the fringe around the whole bag. Then, beginning from that line, draw 4 more lines 1⅜" (3.5cm) apart. Continue to add strips of fringe to cover the bag, placing the sixth, unfringed piece on the very top, even with the top edge.

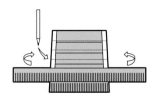

9. Add the grommets: Following the package instructions and using a grommet tool, insert the grommets 1¾" (4.5cm) from each side and ¾" (2cm) down from the top edge.

10. Once the grommets are in place, fringe the top edge, carefully fringing around the grommets but not cutting too close to the hardware.

11. Place "S" hooks through the grommets, hooking them on the outside of the bag. Connect the chains to the hooks, and pinch the top of each "S" closed using a pair of pliers.

12. Open the bag, and push out the pleat to make the bottom of the bag.

"I know women—give them chains, women adore chains."
—Coco Chanel

climbing the walls

climbing the walls

I'm afraid of wallpaper. Don't get me wrong—I actually love the stuff—but I'm nervous to put it on my walls (where it belongs!). What if I get tired of it? Or what if I pick the wrong one? I can't just paint over it like I could with a wall color. But a purse made out of wallpaper? Now that I can commit to. Wallpaper offers so many beautiful patterns and textures. You can make this purse from some leftover scraps or order sample sheets, which cost just a few dollars. The heaviness of wallpaper makes it a particularly good material to work with, and after covering it with strips of clear packing tape, it actually becomes quite durable. Now that I've made several bags out of wallpaper, I'm almost ready to face my walls. . . . On second thought, maybe I'll order a few more samples just to be sure!

finished measurements

2¾" x 10" x 9" (7cm x 25.5cm x 23cm)

supplies

28" x 18" (71cm x 45.5cm) piece of wallpaper (you may need a larger piece if you are trying to isolate a certain pattern)

Clear packing tape

Climbing the Walls pattern template (page 122)

Magnetic snap

½" (13mm) wide double-sided tape

Masking tape

Rotary cutter and self-healing mat (optional)

Ruler

1. "Laminate" the front of the wallpaper by covering it with strips of packing tape placed horizontally, overlapping the strips slightly as you go. Trim the extra tape around the edges, turn the wallpaper over, and repeat on the back.

2. Using the Climbing the Walls pattern template (page 122), cut out the purse shape from the laminated wallpaper, saving the leftover material for the straps.

3. Fold the top edge of the purse shape 1½" (3.8cm) to the inside. Following the package instructions, attach one piece of the magnetic snap in the middle of the flap, 5¾" (14.5cm) from each side and ¾" (2cm) from the top. Repeat on the other flap with the

corresponding part of the snap.

Use a strip of packing tape to hem the flaps.

FOLD

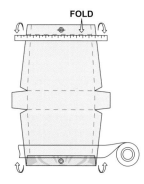

4. Make the straps: Cut four ¾" x 18" (2cm x 45.5cm) strips from the laminated wallpaper left over

from step 1. Use a long, thin strip of double-sided tape to attach 2 wallpaper strips wrong sides together. Use a few pieces of masking tape to hold the strips in place on your cutting surface, and trim the edges so that they're nice and even. (A rotary cutter and self-healing mat work well for this.) Cut an 18" (45.5cm) strip of packing tape, and lay it on your work surface, sticky side up. Lay the double-sided strap down the middle of the tape, and fold the tape edges over to cover and reinforce the strap. Trim the strap to 16½" (42cm) long. Repeat with the other two strips to make the second strap.

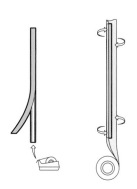

5. Attach the straps to the bag: On the top inside edge of the bag, mark a point 3¼" (8cm) in from each side. Mark another point 3¼" (8cm) in from each side at the bottom of the flap. Line up the *inside* edges of one strap with the marked points on one side of the bag (the strap will be slightly angled). Tape them in place using packing tape (see illo below). Tape them a second time to reinforce. Repeat on the other side of the bag to attach the second strap.

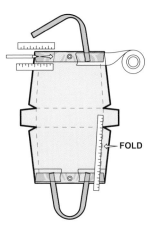

← FOLD

6. Following the fold lines on the Climbing the Walls pattern template (page 122), use a ruler to prefold the bag edges so that the bag will close easily.

7. Close the bag: Fold up the purse so that the side edges overlap slightly and the top side edges overlap each other almost completely. (The side at the top should now measure ¾" [2cm]). Use masking tape to temporarily hold the sides in place. Repeat on the other side. Then make sure the bag is the shape you want. (You may have to adjust the sides a bit so that the bag looks "even".)

8. Once you've taped both sides with masking tape, begin taping one side closed using strips of packing tape, placed *horizontally* and overlapping each other slightly, on the outside of the bag. The clear tape will "disappear" and blend in with the tape you used to laminate the wallpaper. Trim the tape edges flush with the sides so that the tape doesn't extend to the front or back of the bag. Continue taping the entire side, removing the masking tape a section at a time as you go. (Note: Let the top piece of tape [the one near the top edge] bend over slightly on the front and back of the bag. This will help close the narrow top side of the bag securely.) Repeat on the other side, and you're good to go!

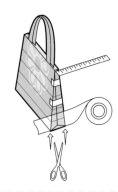

5

small change
stashing small items

If you make only one bag in this book (and I hope you'll make many of them!), make one of the projects from this chapter. You'll get a quick craft fix without too much time or effort, and sometimes a little craftiness is all you need to lift your spirits.

One of my favorite projects in this chapter is the potholder eyeglass case (Hot Pocket, page 88). This is by far the easiest project in the book, and one of the most addictive. (Talk about instant gratification!)

After you make one, you'll want to make a whole drawerful and give them as gifts to everyone you know. In fact, many of these small bags—such as the Face Time coin purse (page 90) and the Eye Candy bag (page 97)—make great presents that can be personalized with the recipient in mind. Not only will your friends and family appreciate their unique gift, you'll have so much fun making it! So, go ahead . . . get crafty. Creating something cute or clever, no matter how small, is good for the soul!

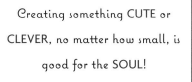

Creating something CUTE or CLEVER, no matter how small, is good for the SOUL!

hot pocket

I don't know about you, but I'm constantly searching for my sunglasses. My friends Debi and Ellen are similarly afflicted, so I made us all personalized glass cases with individualized tags—"Debi's Glasses," "Ellen's Shades," and "Jodi's Specs." Maybe having a pretty labeled case will help us keep our glasses in plain sight!

If you look closely, you'll see that these eyeglass cases started out as potholders. The heavy, quilted fabric is perfect for protecting your sunglasses or delicate frames. Simply fold the potholder in half, and whipstitch the sides with colorful embroidery thread. After making one of these, you'll start to notice all the cute potholders out there just waiting to lend a helping hand.

finished measurements
3½" x 7½" (9cm x 19cm)

supplies
7½" x 7½" (19cm x 19cm) quilted potholder
Personal computer
Fabric transfer paper for inkjet printer (often used for quilting)
Embroidery floss (in coordinating color) and embroidery needle

1. Shape the case: Fold the potholder in half, and pin the sides together.

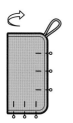

2. Make the tag: Use your computer to design a tag. Print the tag on fabric transfer paper using an inkjet printer. Cut out the tag, remove the backing paper, and fold it in half.

3. Stitch up the sides: Beginning at the bottom corner of the folded potholder, use a long piece of embroidery floss (all 6 strands) to whipstitch the sides together, stopping about 1¾" (4.5cm) from the top edge. Do not tie off thread.

4. Place the tag between the two side edges near the top, and secure it by poking your needle and thread through the potholder front, then through the tag, and finally through the potholder

back. Repeat back and forth until the tag is sewn in.

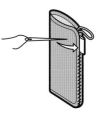

5. When you're done stitching, knot your thread on the inside of the glass case and trim the remaining thread.

face time

Turn a favorite photograph into a sweet little coin purse/key chain that will put a smile on your face all day long. Scan or download a digital photo into your computer, then print the image onto fabric transfer paper using an inkjet printer. Play around with the size of the photo, printing it out on regular paper first until it's the dimension you want.

finished measurements

6½" x 5" (16.5cm x 12.5cm)

supplies

Personal computer

Scanned or digital photograph

Fabric transfer paper for inkjet printer (often used for quilting)

8½" x 14" (21.5cm x 35.5cm) piece lightweight material, such as printed cotton (for lining)

12" (30.5cm) or longer all-purpose polyester zipper

Sewing machine

Thread

7" x 8½" (18cm x 21.5cm) piece heavy material, such as canvas (for back of bag)

6" (15cm) of ⅝" (1.5cm) wide grosgrain ribbon

1" (2.5cm) diameter metal key ring

1. After determining how big you want your image to be (experiment by printing on paper first), print your image on fabric transfer paper using an inkjet printer. Add an extra ½" (13mm) "border" around the image for the seam allowance, and cut out the photo piece. (Note: The bag pictured here was made from a 7½" x 6" [19cm x 15cm] rectangle.) Cut out a back piece from the canvas that measures the same size as the front.

2. Cut 2 pieces from the lining that are the same size as the pieces cut in step 1.

3. Put in the zipper: With the photo fabric right side up, pin the zipper *face down* over the bag front so that the zipper teeth sit ¾" (2cm) from the top edge and the extra zipper length is hanging off each end. Baste using a ½" (13mm) seam allowance and a zipper foot.

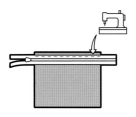

4. With right sides together, pin one lining piece to the front (photo) piece, keeping the edges even. Stitch the upper edges together using a ½" (13mm) seam allowance and a zipper foot.

5. Turn the front piece right side out; gently press, ironing mostly on the lining side to

avoid marring the photo image. Using a ¼" (6mm) seam allowance, topstitch the upper edge of the front near the zipper.

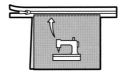

6. Apply the zipper to the back and the back lining in the same manner.

7. Turn the piece right side out, and press gently, again ironing mostly on the lining side to protect the photo. Using a ¼" (6mm) seam allowance, topstitch the upper edge near the zipper, just as you did on the front.

8. Prepare the key ring loop: Fold the grosgrain ribbon in half, and baste together 1½" (3.8cm) from the fold.

9. Place the ribbon loop on one side front of the bag, lining up the stitch line with the bag edge and

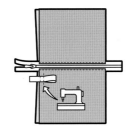

orienting the fold toward the center. (The loop should be about ¾" [2cm] from the top of the bag.) Baste into place using a ⅜" (1cm) seam allowance.

10. With the zipper three-quarters open, fold the bag in half so that the right sides are together. Pin the side and bottom edges together. Using a ½" (13mm) seam allowance, stitch the front and back sections together at the sides and lower edge. Stitch back and forth several times over the zipper on both ends to create a "stop."

11. Clip the bottom corners on a diagonal, and trim the sides and bottom edges to ¼" (6mm). Cut off the extra zipper and ribbon lengths, and trim all threads. Zigzag the raw edges together around the bag to finish them. Turn the bag right side out, and add the key ring to the ribbon loop.

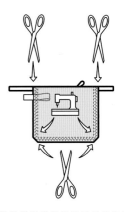

play money

Add some levity to the dreary task of paying bills with a checkbook cover made from Monopoly money. Clear packing tape "laminates" the fabric, which is made of alternating rows of white $1 bills with pink $5 bills. For those big spenders out there, try combining blue $50 bills with gold $500 bills. Check writing has never been so much fun—just be careful not to break the bank!

Note that your needle may get sticky when sewing through the tape. Make sure to wipe it as you go (using a dry paper towel) to keep your stitches and needle on the money.

finished measurements
6½" x 3¾" (16.5cm x 9.5cm), closed
6½" x 7½" (16.5cm x 19cm), open

supplies
Clear packing tape
Monopoly money (24 bills to make the case)
6½" x 13½" (16.5cm x 34.5cm) rectangle cut from paper
Sewing machine and thread (or clear cellophane tape, ¾" [2cm] wide)

1. Make the Monopoly "fabric": Begin with a strip of packing tape, approximately 18" (46cm) long, sticky side up. Place a row of 3 Monopoly bills, face down and overlapping one another slightly, on the sticky tape. Flip the 3-bill layer over, and add another strip of packing tape. Flip the layer over again, and add another row of 3 bills. Then cover the back of the first row of bills with a strip of packing tape. Keep repeating this process, layering the tape and the bills and flipping the fabric back and forth as needed, until you have completed 8 rows. Trim the tape around the fabric outline to neaten the edges. (Note: Laminating the paper is a little tricky. The paper money is not forgiving, so you can't reposition it once you lay it down on the sticky tape. If you make a mistake—as I did several times—just cut off the bad row and add on from there.)

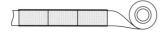

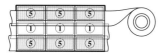

2. Using the 6½" x 13½" (16.5cm x 34.5cm) paper rectangle as your guide, cut out your "fabric" on a diagonal.

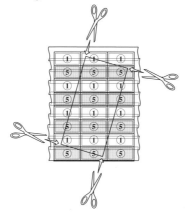

3. "Finish" the bottom and top edges by covering them with a piece of packing tape folded lengthwise over the raw edges. Trim the extra tape.

4. Form the checkbook case: Fold over the top and bottom edges of the Monopoly "fabric" piece toward the back 3" (7.5cm) on each end. Use a piece of masking tape to temporarily hold the edges in place.

5. Close the side seams: Stitch ⅛" (3mm) from the edge, backstitching at the beginning and end of the seam. *Or,* fold a long strip of cellophane tape over the side edges. Remove the masking tape, and insert your checkbook and register!

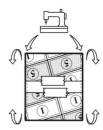

mo' money

You probably don't want to raid your family's Monopoly game to make the Play Money checkbook cover. So where can you get your hands on more money? Check out garage sales and thrift stores for old games. Or shop online for Monopoly replacement money. You can get a whole new pack of bills for just a few bucks. If only it were that easy to refill our real bank accounts!

campy coin purse

It should come as no shock to learn that one of my favorite activities at camp as a kid was Arts and Crafts—leather crafts, in particular. And this Campy Coin Purse is based on an old Tandy Leathercraft coin purse kit. My modern version is a little bigger and fatter and is made out of shiny heavyweight patent leather vinyl. Instead of leather laces, a bright plastic lanyard lace (also a throwback to camp) ties things together.

Of course, at camp, the leather coin purse pieces were precut and the holes were already punched. You'll have to work a little harder this time around. But actually, using a hollow steel punch and hammer to make the holes is quite therapeutic! I enjoyed it so much that there may even be a pair of patent leather moccasins in my future.

finished measurements

2⅛" x 5" x 2½" (5.3cm x 12.5cm x 6.5cm)

supplies

Campy Purse Body and Gusset pattern templates (page 123)

9" x 9" (23cm x 23cm) piece patent leather or plain vinyl with fabric backing (often used for upholstery; heavier than plain patent leather vinyl)

Dressmaker's tracing paper or pencil

³⁄₃₂" (2.3mm) steel punch (sometimes referred to as a "hollow steel punch" or "dry punch") (see Resources, page 116)

Hammer or wood mallet

Cardboard or a plastic (or "poly") cutting board

Sewing machine

Thread (to match vinyl)

7" (18cm) all-purpose polyester zipper (in contrasting color)

⅛" (3mm) wide double-sided "basting" tape (available at fabric stores)

Masking tape

1 skein plastic lanyard laces (to match zipper)

campy coin purse

1. Trace the Campy Purse Body and Gusset pattern templates (page 123) onto the *back* of the fabric, marking the holes and zipper line. (Note: Transfer the marks from the template to the fabric by using dressmaker's tracing paper or by covering the back of your paper pattern with pencil and then placing the pattern on the fabric and tracing over all the markings.)

2. Carefully cut out the pattern pieces, keeping the edges as smooth as possible.

3. On the gusset piece, cut out the center of the strap, leaving the strap attached at one end.

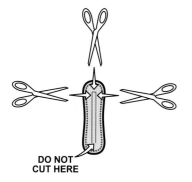

DO NOT CUT HERE

4. Punch holes in both purse pieces using a hollow steel punch and a hammer (or mallet). Place several pieces of cardboard or a plastic cutting board underneath to protect your table.

5. Make the strap: With the gusset face down, fold the strap back to make a loop. Stitch in place.

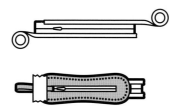

6. Put in the zipper: On the *front* of the zipper, place thin strips of double-sided basting tape on the very edges of the zipper tape. Then position the zipper in the opening on the gusset left by the strap, with the zipper pull at the end near the strap. (Use a piece of masking tape to temporarily hold the strap out of the way.)

7. Sew in the zipper: Using a ¼" (6mm) seam allowance and a zipper foot, sew in the zipper on the wrong side of the gusset. Begin sewing at the top of the zipper, and sew all the way around, backstitching at the beginning and end to secure. (Use a pin to mark your seam line at the

bottom of the zipper, ¼" [6mm] from the bottom front opening.) Trim the extra zipper length.

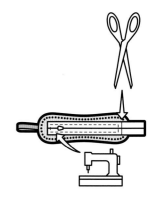

8. Lace up the coin purse: Locate the starting hole on the purse body (marked on the template). Fold the body in half, keeping the starting hole in the center of the fold. Do not crease the fabric; cup it (as if it were a taco shell).

Match up the starting hole on the gusset with the starting hole on the body. Start to lace, leaving 6" (15cm) of lanyard lace on the inside, to be tied off later.

Continue stitching the pieces together. When you get to the end, tie off the laces on the inside, knot them several times, and trim the extra lanyard.

flashback

Founded in 1919 in Fort Worth, Texas, Tandy Leather Company (originally called the Hinckley-Tandy Leather Company after its two owners, Norton Hinckley and Dave L. Tandy) sold leather shoe parts, such as soles, heels, and shoelaces, to local shoe repair shops. The company nearly went under during World War II, when shoes were rationed in the United States—adults were allowed just two pairs of shoes per year—and leather for other civilian uses all but evaporated.

That's when Dave Tandy's son, Charles, came to the rescue. While serving in the Navy during the war, Charles observed how military hospitals used leathercraft as therapy for patients and how the soldiers and sailors enjoyed working with leather as a form of recreation. Charles suggested that leathercraft would be a way for the company to branch out and sustain itself during the lean war years. The new focus on the hobby category proved extremely successful. Now the biggest company of its kind, Tandy is generally credited with teaching the world how to "leathercraft."

A "modern" leathercraft kit from the 1960s.

eye candy

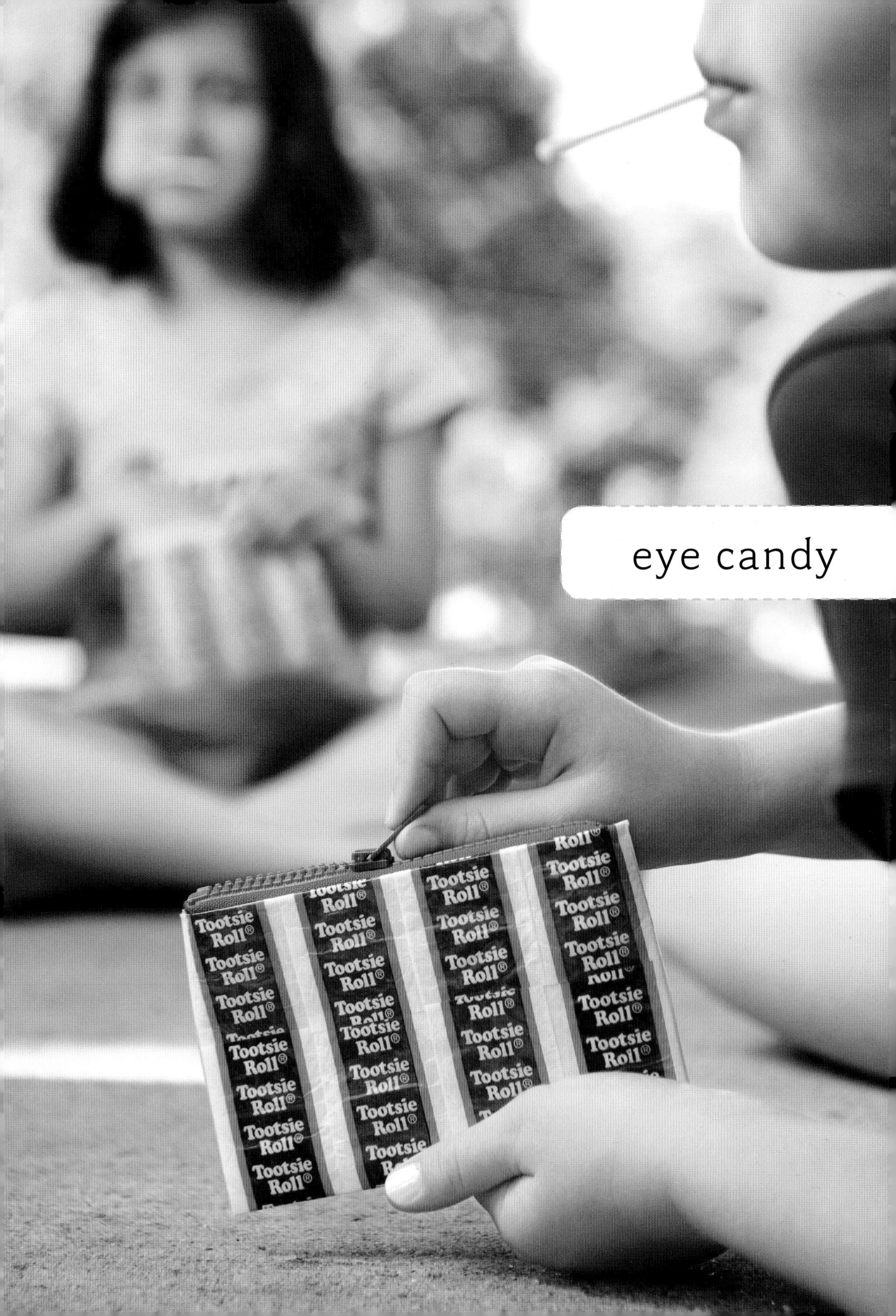

eye candy

These no-sew candy wrapper coin purses are really fun to make, and they're popular with both kids and adults. But if you've got a sweet tooth, they can be dangerous. The good news: You'll have plenty of "volunteers" eager to help you unwrap the sweets. Everyone needs a little candy now and then!

finished measurements

5½" x 4⅛" (14cm x 10.5cm)

supplies

2 to 3 dozen candies in wax wrappers (such as Tootsie Rolls, Starbursts, Mary Janes, Bit-O-Honeys, Tootsie Pops, and Double Bubble or Bazooka bubble gum)

Clear packing tape

Heavyweight plastic zipper, any length (for this project, I used a size 5 zipper from Steinlauf and Stoller [see Resources, page 116])

Stapler and staples

Duct tape

Clear cellophane tape, ¾" (2cm) wide

1. Remove the candies from their wrappers. (Note: This can be grueling work that may require eating many of the candies to keep your strength up.)

2. Prepare the candy wrappers by folding each one into a uniform size. (Note: I wrapped and creased them around a piece of narrow cardboard to ensure that all the wrappers were about the same dimensions and showed colorful surfaces on the front and back.) Then arrange them in the pattern you want.

3. Make the "fabric" by layering and laminating the wrappers using strips of packing tape. Begin with a long strip of packing tape, sticky side up. Place a few rows of wrappers on the tape, and cover them with another piece of packing tape. Continue layering the wrappers and tape, flipping the fabric over and then back as you go, alternating the tape and the wrappers until the wrappers are "laminated" on both sides with several strips of tape. Continue until you have about a 5½" x 9" (14cm x 23cm) piece of fabric (the actual size will vary depending on what wrappers you use).

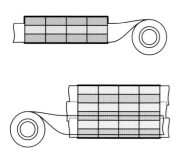

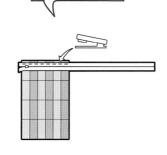

8. Close one side of the bag: Fold the bag in half, and close the zipper. Once your bag has taken shape, open the zipper slightly and pinch the edges on that side together so that they meet perfectly. Carefully tape the edges on the first side closed with a folded piece of cellophane tape.

6. Open up the zipper, and apply the other zipper half to the other side of the bag in the same manner.

4. "Finish" the long sides of the fabric by folding a piece of packing tape over the edges. Trim the extra tape all around.

9. To close the second side, first close the zipper all the way. Cut the zipper to shorten it (but leave an extra 2" [5cm]). "Finish" the cut end with a folded piece of cellophane or duct tape. Tuck the extra zipper inside, and tape the open side as you did the first side.

5. Put in the zipper: Lay the fabric right side up, with the short ends at the top and bottom. Pin the zipper face down on the right side of the fabric so that the top edge is ⅞" (2.2cm) from the zipper teeth and the zipper pull is ¼" (6mm) from the left side edge. Staple in the zipper, using a ½" (13mm) seam allowance (and opening the zipper as you go to keep the zipper tape flat).

7. Fold the zipper back at the staples, and push it flat to form a clean seam. On the wrong side of the fabric, hold the zipper down with a piece of duct tape that measures ¼" (6mm) shorter than each side. Repeat on the other side of the zipper.

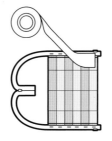

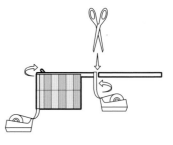

6

on the go
bags that will take you places

One of the best things about making your own bags (or making *anything*, for that matter) is the opportunity to get your creative juices flowing. Once you start exercising that creative part of your brain, your whole mind opens up to new things and you see inspiration everywhere you look. In this chapter, I found my inspiration in a child's game (Twist It, Sister!, page 102), a yellow rain slicker (Bungee Bag, page 105) a strip of packing tape (Rush!, page 108) and, finally, a piece of grassy green Astroturf (Life's a Picnic, page 112).

The projects in this chapter are more challenging than some of the others in this book, mostly because they are made out of unusual materials. But the patterns are actually pretty simple. These bag shapes can be created from any fabric, so if something inspires you, try it out. Look at old things in new ways (the ultimate form of recycling!), and don't be afraid to add a touch of whimsy or humor to your projects.

Speaking of having fun, check out my ideas for a homemade bag luncheon ("Bag Lunch," page 111). Think of it as the new sewing circle (or, in this case, the no-sewing circle). Inviting friends over for a bite to eat and some crafty fun is a great way to spend a Sunday afternoon or to celebrate a special occasion, such as a birthday or engagement. Your friends will thank you for tapping into their creative sides. And once you get that motor started, there's no stopping it. You won't believe where your creativity can take you—the journey is positively (and simply) sublime!

twist it, sister!

This bag is all about putting a new twist on an old thing. It's made from a Twister board game mat, folded in half for extra durability. My son and daughter love this oversized tote, and although I made it as a beach bag, it's been used to carry pillows and pajamas to sleepovers and to haul sports equipment all over town. Once people figure out what it's made from, a smile creeps across their faces. I think it conjures up the kid in all of us—and the desire to hang out and have a good time.

The bag is constructed very much like the Original No-Sew Tote in Chapter 2 (page 36), but it's a little trickier because of the dot pattern and size of the bag. Stick with it. You may get a little twisted up in the process, but the results will make you feel like a winner!

finished measurements
8½" x 23½" x 17" (21.5cm x 59.5cm x 43cm)

supplies
Vinyl play mat from a Twister board game
Hair dryer
Masking tape
48" (122cm) of 2" (5cm) wide nylon webbing
Stapler and staples
White duct tape

1. Before cutting out the fabric, use a hair dryer to "iron" out the wrinkles on your Twister game mat by blowing hot air over the creases. Hold the hair dryer at least 12" (30.5cm) from the mat. You won't be able to get *all* the wrinkles out, but this will help. (Note: An iron will ruin the vinyl.)

2. Fold the game mat in half so that all four colored dots are visible. Then fold the mat in half again, so that the red and blue dots are on one side and the yellow and green dots are on the other.

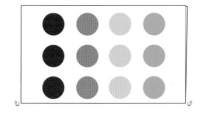

3. Hold the folded mat up to the light and line up the circles, with the red and blue circle side facing the front. Use a piece of masking tape to temporarily hold the mat together. Orient the folded mat so that the red circles run across the top. Keeping the fold at the bottom and centering the dots, cut the mat so that it measures 24½" x 26" (62cm x 66cm). (Note: You will be trimming both the sides and the top of the fabric but keeping the fabric at the bottom folded. You will end up with two pieces of folded fabric with wrong sides together—an outside piece and a "lining." Part of the side dots will be trimmed off.)

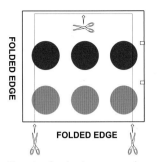

FOLDED EDGE

4. Keeping both pieces together (with wrong sides together), open up the fabric. Fold over the top edges (near the red dots) about 4½" (11.5cm), making sure the circles on the front of the bag fabric stay lined up with those on the lining fabric. Use pieces of masking tape to temporarily hold the folded edges in place. Repeat on the other end, near the green circles.

5. Cut two 24" (61cm) straps from the nylon webbing. Place one strap along one end of the fabric, 8¼" (21cm) in from each side, angled slightly, so that the finished, exposed strap measures 16½" (42cm). Using plenty of sta-

ples, staple the strap to the inside folded flap, stapling only through the strap and the flap, so that the staples do not show through what will eventually be the front of the bag. Repeat on the other end, making sure the front strap lines up with the back strap.

6. Once the straps have been stapled into place, cover the staples with 3 lengths of duct tape to securely "hem" the top of the bag. Repeat on the other end.

7. Staple the sides together: With right sides together, fold the rectangle, lining up the sides and handles of the bag. Use a few pieces of masking tape to temporarily hold the sides together. Staple each side of the bag using a ½" (13mm) seam allowance. Make sure the staples are very close together to create a straight, clean line. Once you have stapled the sides, cover the staples with a

long piece of duct tape (folded lengthwise over the raw edge).

8. Create the bottom: With the bag still inside out, flatten one corner to create a triangular point, aligning the side seam with the center bottom of the bag. Draw an 8½" (21.5cm) line 4¼" (11cm) from the point. Staple along the line. Repeat on the other side.

9. Trim the corners to ½" (13mm), and cover with a piece of duct tape (folded lengthwise).

10. Turn the bag right side out, and head to the pool!

bungee bag

The challenge of making a cool tote bag out of items found solely at the hardware store was alluring. My inspiration came when I spotted a man's protective suit made from bright yellow PVC material. The extra-large rain slicker cost less than $10 and provided enough fabric for several bags. After adding grommets, I pinched the bungee cord straps in place using ordinary pliers. This happy yellow carryall is waterproof and is sure to add a little sunshine to a rainy day.

finished measurements
6" x 20" x 14" (15cm x 51cm x 35.5cm)

supplies
PVC protective suit, size extra-large

1½" wide yellow duct tape

Masking tape

Stapler and staples

Iron and ironing board

Four ⅜" (9mm) diameter grommets

Grommet tool (or grommet pliers)

Hole punch

Two 18" (45.5cm) bungee cords

Pliers

Masking tape

1. Cut out the body of the bag: Lay the coat flat, with the snaps closed and the arms spread open. Cut off the sleeves and collar by cutting straight across from underarm to underarm (keep the bottom section of the coat to work with in this step, and reserve one sleeve for making the bag bottom). Unsnap the jacket bottom, and fold the fabric in half so that the snaps are now all on one edge. Making sure the coat's side seams are centered, cut out two 21" x 14" (53.5cm x 35.5cm) pieces for the main body of the bag by cutting through both layers of the coat at the same time. (Note: The finished bottom edge of the coat will be the *top* of the bag, and the snapped edge will be cut off.)

2. Cut out the bag bottom: Using one sleeve (as is, with two layers of fabric), cut out a 15" x 7½"

(38cm x 19 cm) rectangle along one fold of the sleeve, keeping the fold at the top.

3. Reinforce the top of the main bag panels: Even though the top edge is already "finished," place a strip of duct tape on the wrong side of the front panel, all the way across and ½" (13mm) down from the finished top edge of the bag (see illustration below). (Note: This will help reinforce the fabric for the grommets, which will be put in later.) Repeat for the back panel.

4. Staple the main panels together: With right sides facing, use masking tape to hold the two main panels together as you work. Staple the *sides* of the bag together using a ½" (13mm) seam allowance (the bottom will be attached later). Remove the masking tape as you go.

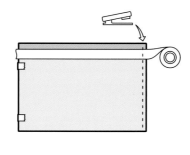

5. Use an unplugged, cold iron to press the side seams flat. (Note: Do *not* use a heated iron—it will melt the fabric!) Cover the flattened seams with duct tape. Trim the tape at the bottom and top edges to neaten them. Repeat on the other side of the bag.

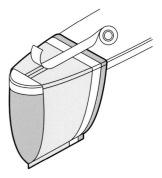

6. Attach the bottom: At the bottom of the main bag, mark a point 2½" (6.5cm) in from each side. Place one long edge of the bottom panel (still doubled, with right sides facing out) on the bottom edge of the bag, between the two marked points on one side of the bag. Lining up the raw edges of the main panel with the raw edges of the bottom panel, pin the bottom panel in place (place the pins in the seam allowance to avoid leaving pinholes in the finished bag). (Note:

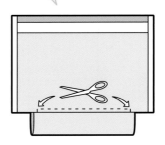

The bag bottom panel is still a *folded, double layer* of fabric. This helps reinforce the bottom of the finished bag.)

7. Staple the bottom in place: Starting and stopping ½" (13mm) from each side of the bottom panel, staple the bag bottom to the main panel using a ½" (13mm) seam allowance. Attach the opposite edge in the same manner.

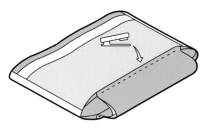

8. Make a ½" (13mm) clip in the bottom edge of the main panel only, cutting up into the seam allowance to meet the *end of the seam line*. (This clip will allow the bottom corner to turn easily.) Repeat on the other end. Repeat again on the back main panel of the bag.

9. Make the bottom sides: Pin the short edge of the bottom panel to the main panel, lining up the raw edges. Staple the seam between the clips using a ½" (13mm) seam allowance. Join the opposite end of the bottom panel in the same way. Trim the corners at a 45-degree angle, being careful not to cut too close.

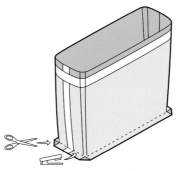

10. Cover the bag bottom edges with tape: Turn the bag inside out over the arm of your ironing board. Using an unplugged, cold iron, press all the seams toward the top of the bag, and cover each section with duct tape, folded over th-

bottom and up the sides. Trim diagonally at the corners to neaten up the tape. Press the tape down to make sure it is flat and secure.

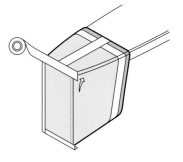

11. Put in the grommets: Mark a point 6½" (16.5cm) in from each side and ¾" (2cm) down from the top edge. Following the package instructions, insert the grommets.

12. Attach the bungee straps: The straps on this bag are made from 18" (45.5cm) bungee cords (which actually measure 19" [48.5cm] from hook end to hook end), but you can use any length you want. Hook the bungee straps through the grommets, with the point of the hooks facing inside. Wrap the hooks with masking tape to protect them, and then close the hooks using pliers. Remove the masking tape.

finished measurements

4" x 14¼" x 11" (10cm x36cm x 28cm)

supplies

55 yd (50m) roll printed "RUSH" packing tape

60 yd (54m) roll duct tape (in matching color)

Rush! Messenger Bag pattern templates: Front, Back, and Bottom Panel (pages 124–125)

Stapler and staples

8' (2.4m) of 2" (5cm) wide nylon webbing

Lighter or matches

2" (5cm) wide plastic buckle

Sewing machine

Thread (to match nylon webbing)

rush!

Like the fabric for the Caution! bag in Chapter 1 (page 31), this bag is made from "RUSH" packing tape layered over duct tape. The resulting material has an industrial, heavy-duty look and feel, just right for a utilitarian messenger bag. The adjustable strap loops through the entire bag, giving it added support, and fastens with a plastic belt buckle from the hardware store. Making the fabric for this bag will take some time, but hang in there. After all, what's the rush?

1. Make four pieces of "RUSH" fabric in the following dimensions:

    1 piece: 18" x 15" (45.5cm x 38cm)

    1 piece: 18" x 33" (45.5cm x 84cm)

    2 pieces: 24" x 5½" (61cm x 14cm).

    To make the fabric, place a long piece of duct tape (about 18" [45.5cm] or 24" [61cm] long, depending on which piece you're making) on your work surface, sticky side up. Cut a piece of "RUSH" tape about the same length, and place it sticky side *down* on the duct tape. (Make sure the words are somewhat centered.) Flip the fabric over, and add another strip of duct tape, overlapping the first strip. Continue layering the duct tape with "RUSH" tape, flipping the fabric over and back as you go.

2. Once you've made your fabric pieces, use the three Messenger Bag pattern templates (pages 124–125) to cut out the bag pieces. Center the words to your liking. (Note: On the back piece, "RUSH" should be upside down so that it will be right side up when you flip over the bag flap.)

3. On the front and back pieces, mark the center middle on the bottom seam line (see illustration for step 6).

4. Prepare the bottom panel: With the right sides together, pin the two bottom panel pieces together on one of the short sides (making sure you like how the words read). Staple the pieces together using a ½" (13mm) seam

allowance. Press the seam open flat with your hand, and cover it with duct tape.

5. Fold over each short end of the bottom panel 2½" (6.5cm), and cover the "hems" with 2 strips of duct tape each.

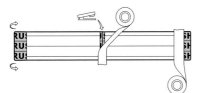

6. Fold over the top edge of the bag front piece 2½" (6.5cm), and hold the "hem" in place with 2 strips of duct tape.

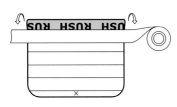

7. On the wrong side of the bottom panel, draw a ½" (13mm) seam allowance along each long side.

8. With *right* sides together, pin the bottom panel to the bag front piece, matching up the center mark on the front with the center seam on the bottom panel.

Snip around the curves on the bottom panel, within the seam allowance, to ease the corners.

9. Staple the bottom panel to the bag front piece, using the drawn line as your guide for a ½" (13mm) seam allowance and removing the pins as you go.

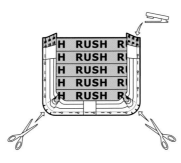

10. Attach the bottom panel to the bag back piece in the same manner, matching up the center bottom mark with the bottom panel center seam.

11. Clip the top front corners on a diagonal, and cover all seams with duct tape (folded lengthwise over the raw edge). Use small pieces of tape around the curves.

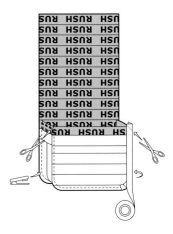

12. Turn the bag right side out. To make the flap, fold over the extra fabric on the back 9" (23cm), with *right sides together*. Staple the flap sides together using a ½" (13mm) seam allowance. (Note: The seams do not need to be

in the bag

"Messenger" bags were first produced from heavy canvas and made for telephone linemen (not messengers) in New York City in the 1950s. Bicycle messengers in Manhattan started using the bags in the 1970s because of their simple, sturdy design. Nowadays, everyone from Kate Spade to Prada has co-opted the clean-lined messenger-style bag, establishing it as a new "classic" purse shape.

reinforced with duct tape.) Trim the corners on a diagonal, and carefully turn the flap right side out, pushing out the corners.

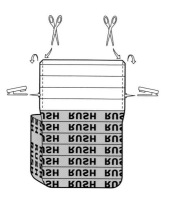

13. Add the straps: Cut a 92½" (235cm) strap from the nylon webbing. Use a lighter or matches to "finish" the edges of the straps by quickly and carefully passing the flame back and forth over the ends. (Note: This works only with nylon or polypropylene webbing, *not* with cotton straps.)

14. Carefully mark 10 slits on the bag around the sides and bottom, following the guidelines from the bag bottom pattern template. Note: The first slit is 1" (2.5cm) from the top.

15. Using small, sharp scissors, cut the slits 2" (5cm) wide.

bag lunch

What better way for you and your friends to "get your craft on" than by throwing a bag luncheon? Just whip up some cute purse invitations, designed on your computer and decorated with fabric on the front. After lunch is served, you can provide your guests with material and directions for making an easy no-sew bag. Ask your guests to B.Y.O.S. (Bring Your Own Stapler)—unless you happen to have a dozen of them lying around the house!

16. Thread one end of the strap through the end of the buckle without the prongs, fold the end over about 3" (7.5cm), and machine-stitch to secure, reinforcing the stitching.

17. Thread the strap through all the slits and then through the plastic prong. Snap the buckle shut, and adjust the straps to your desired length.

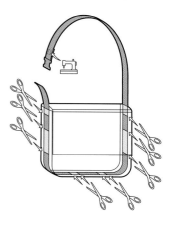

life's a picnic

If you're up for a challenge, set aside a cloudy weekend to tackle this Astroturf picnic basket. The bag itself is actually pretty simple, but working with the Astroturf is, well, no picnic! It makes a big mess and is hard to sew on (you have to use a walking foot attachment for your machine to feed this thick material). I lined the bag with red-and-white-checkered oilcloth, but a vinyl tablecloth would work well, too.

Although this bag takes some time and perseverance, the results will make all the hard work worthwhile. After all, life isn't always a picnic. So when the sun is shining, grab your picnic basket and seize the moment. Kick back, relax, and let the sunshine in!

finished measurements

8" x 20" x 14" (20.5cm x51cm x 35.5cm)

supplies

Astroturf (buy a precut piece, 6' x 9' [1.8m x 2.7m] or have a piece cut off the roll, 4' x 12' [1.2m x 3.6m])

8" x 10" (20.5cm x 25.5cm) piece thick (16-gauge) clear plastic covering

Sewing machine

Green thread

48" x 48" (122cm x 122cm) piece oilcloth (or similar-sized vinyl tablecloth) (for lining)

Iron and ironing board (optional)

Two 14" (35.5cm) premade leather handles

Stapler and staples

19" x 35" (48.5cm x 89cm) piece heavy-duty interfacing

Duct tape (any color)

Plastic silverware

Note: Because of the thick fabric, use a ⅝" (1.5cm) seam allowance on this bag unless otherwise instructed. Use a walking foot attachment when sewing all parts of this bag, including the plastic pocket, the main bag, and the lining.

1. Using regular heavy-duty scissors, *not* your good fabric shears, cut out the Astroturf in the following sizes, making sure the "grain" of the grass is horizontal:

   Main bag piece: 20¾" x 37½" (52.5cm x 95cm)

   Side panels (cut 2): 8½" x 15¾" (21.5cm x 40cm).

2. From the clear plastic covering, cut an 8¾" x 6" (22cm x 15cm) piece for the pocket.

3. Pin the pocket onto the front of the main bag piece, centering it 6" (15cm) down from the top edge. Topstitch the sides and bottom of the pocket using a ¼" (6mm) seam allowance and backstitching at the beginning and end of the seam to secure. Make sure to leave the top open.

4. Using a pencil and a ruler, mark 2 seam lines on the pocket to make three 2¾" (7cm) wide sections. Stitch on the seam lines, backstitching at the beginning and end of the seams to secure.

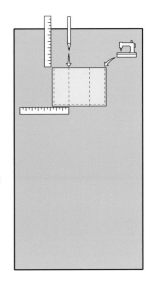

5. Attach the sides: On the wrong side of the fabric, mark the middle bottom of one side panel (this should be 4¾" [12cm] in from each edge). Mark halfway down the side of the main bag piece (18¼" [46.5cm] from the top). With *right* sides together, pin the side panel to the main bag piece, lining up the center marks. Sew along the edge using a ⅝" (1.5cm) seam allowance and starting and stopping ⅝" (1.5cm) from the side panel edges.

CENTER

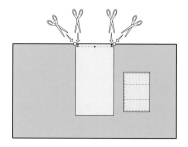

6. Clip small, ⅝" x ⅝" (1.5cm x 1.5cm) squares on the corners of the side panel (as shown below). On the main bag, clip up ⅝" (1.5cm) into the seam allowance.

7. Pin the side seams together. Stitch the seams using a ⅝" (1.5cm) seam allowance. Repeat on the other edge. Attach the second side panel to the other side in the same manner.

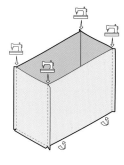

8. Cut out the lining: From the oilcloth or tablecloth, cut 2 main pieces, each measuring 20¾" x 19⅜" (52.5cm x 49cm). Also cut 2 side pieces, each measuring 8½" x 15¾" (21.5cm x 40cm).

9. Assemble the lining: With *right* sides together, pin the two main lining pieces together along the bottom edge. Using a ⅝" (1.5cm) seam allowance, sew 3" (7.5cm) on both sides, leaving an opening large enough to turn the bag through later. Open the fabric up, and press the seams open flat using your hands or an unplugged, cold iron.

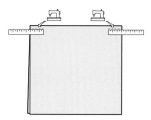

10. As with the Astroturf in step 5, mark the middle bottom of the lining side panels (this should be 4¾" [12cm] in from each side). With right sides together, pin the lining side panel to the main bag panel, lining up the center mark with the seam. Sew along the edge using a ⅝" (1.5cm) seam allowance and starting and stopping ⅝" (1.5cm) from the edges. Clip and stitch the rest of the lining in the same manner as with the Astroturf (following steps 6 through 8).

11. Attach the handles: With the lining still inside out, attach the handles to the *inside* of the lining so that the loops of the handles hang down. Place the handles about 6" (15cm) in from each side, and use a few staples to "baste" them into place ½" (13mm) from the edge.

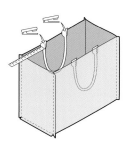

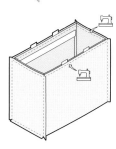

smoothing out the Astroturf and lining as you go. Place the plastic silverware in the front pocket.

12. Add interfacing to the Astroturf bag: Cut a 35" x 19" (89cm x 48.5cm) piece of interfacing. Use duct tape to attach the interfacing to the wrong side of the Astroturf bag. The interfacing should sit between the side seams and about 1¼" (3cm) from the top edge. Make sure the duct tape is not in the top edge seam allowance.

14. Turn the bag right side out through the opening in the lining. Slipstitch or machine-stitch the opening in the lining closed. Insert the lining into the bag,

15. Roll out your picnic blanket, and relax. You've made it to the end!

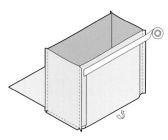

13. Attach the lining to the bag: With right sides together (and wrong sides facing out), pin the lining to the bag (over the handles), lining up the side seams and keeping the upper raw edges even. Stitch along the upper edge of the bag using a ⅝" (1.5cm) seam allowance.

resources

fabrics

B&J FABRICS

www.bandjfabrics.com

This family-run fabric store in Manhattan—a mainstay in the garment district for more than sixty years—is also open to the public. They carry just about every type of fabric imaginable, including a terrific selection of purse-weight material, such as the patent leather vinyl used for projects in this book.

REPRODEPOT FABRICS

www.reprodepot.com

You'll get a lot of ideas just browsing this online fabric store, with its terrific collection of vintage reproduction and retro-themed textiles. Their staff is really nice, too!

DENVER FABRICS

www.denverfabrics.com

This giant fabric store is a great source for oilcloth and tons of other fabrics and supplies, most sold at discount prices. Shop online or at their store in Littleton, Colorado.

PURL PATCHWORK

www.purlsoho.com

Sisters Joelle and Jennifer Hoverson opened this sumptuous fabric store in 2006 as the counterpart to their yarn shop, Purl, in downtown Manhattan. The shop specializes in fabrics made from natural fibers and has a homey, creative feel. Their online shop is very manageable and carries a great selection of printed fabrics.

OILCLOTH INTERNATIONAL

www.oilcloth.com

This is one of the largest wholesale distributors and manufacturers of oilcloth in the United States. The company does not sell retail, but they are happy to help you find a store in your area that stocks their beautiful patterns of oilcloth.

notions and trimmings

THE SNAP SOURCE

www.snapsource.com

This company's cool long-prong snaps are incredibly easy to put in and come in a huge variety of styles, colors, and sizes. The owner, Jeanine Twig, is completely hands-on and full of great ideas. You can buy the snaps in fabric stores or place an order online. Stock up!

M&J TRIMMING

www.mjtrim.com

Shelves of ribbons reach to the ceiling in this vast trimmings store. They also carry a very good supply of buttons and purse handles. If you can't make it to NYC, you can find almost everything you need on their Web site.

STEINLAUF AND STOLLER

www.steinlaufandstoller.com

This old-time sewing supply store stocks everything from zippers to bra cups. Their online catalog shows thousands of items stocked for immediate delivery.

purse supplies

TALL POPPY CRAFT PRODUCTS

www.tallpoppycraft.com

Check out this website if you're looking for purse supplies, such as handles, straps, or magnetic snaps. The company is based in Sydney, Australia.

LACIS

www.lacis.com

Located in Berkeley, California, Lacis is a store, museum, and school where patrons can shop while learning everything about lace and other textile arts. The online shop is a wonderful resource for purse supplies, such as handles and purse frames.

other supplies and information

DUCK TAPE CLUB

www.ducktapeclub.com

Make this your first stop when searching out anything to do with duct tape. The "club" is part of Duck Brand Duct Tape's Web site, which is loaded with information about my favorite sticky adhesive and can recommend a retailer near you that stocks the exact shade you're looking for. The site also offers a limited array of colors for online purchase.

THERM O WEB

www.thermoweb.com

Visit Thermo O Web's online site to shop for all sorts of cool craft products, including the iron-on vinyl used for the Shower Power purse (page 64).

ULINE

www.uline.com

Run by the Uihlein family, this company is one of the largest shipping supply sources in the United States. You'll find every kind of tape imaginable, in every color under the sun. Browse through their extensive catalog or shop online. The company also offers same-day shipping.

THE CONTAINER STORE

www.containerstore.com

Even if you're not looking to get organized, you'll get lots of ideas from this store, which bills itself as the "neatest site on the web." The metallic bubble envelope used for The Envelope, Please purse (page 76) is available at the company's retail shops or by phone at 1-888-CONTAIN (but not online).

THE BUZZARD BRAND

www.thebuzzardbrand.com

Retro charms (for example, see Charmed, I'm Sure on page 19) and a lot of other cool stuff can be found on this site. Proprietor and crafter Laura Stokes makes a lot of the items herself in her California studio.

IKEA

www.ikea.com

When hunting for great-looking fabrics and textiles at affordable prices, you really can't beat this design store for the masses. There's always something new and inspiring in the store or catalog, and many items can be purchased online.

TANDY LEATHER FACTORY

www.tandyleatherfactory.com

Shop here for all sorts of leather-working tools, such as the hollow steel punch and wooden mallet used to make the Campy Coin Purse (page 94). Browse around; you never know what you'll find!

templates

The following templates will need to be photocopied and enlarged to the appropriate size before you pin them to your fabric. In small quantities, for personal use, you are free to make photocopies from this book.

shower curtain tote
photocopy at 333% magnification

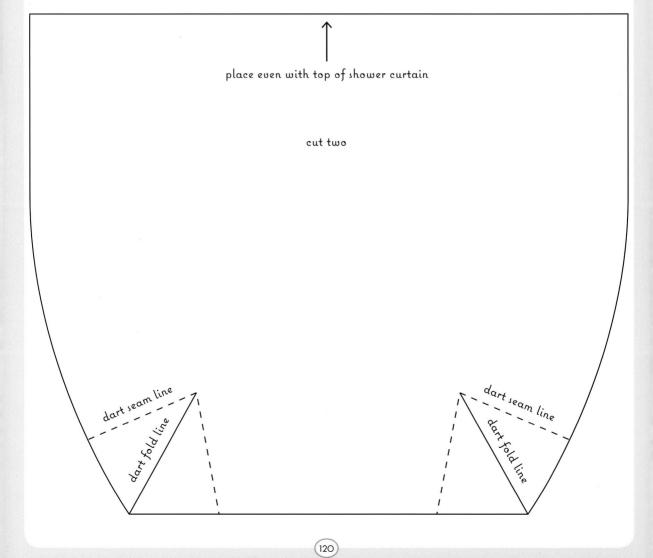

place even with top of shower curtain

cut two

dart seam line

dart fold line

dart seam line

dart fold line

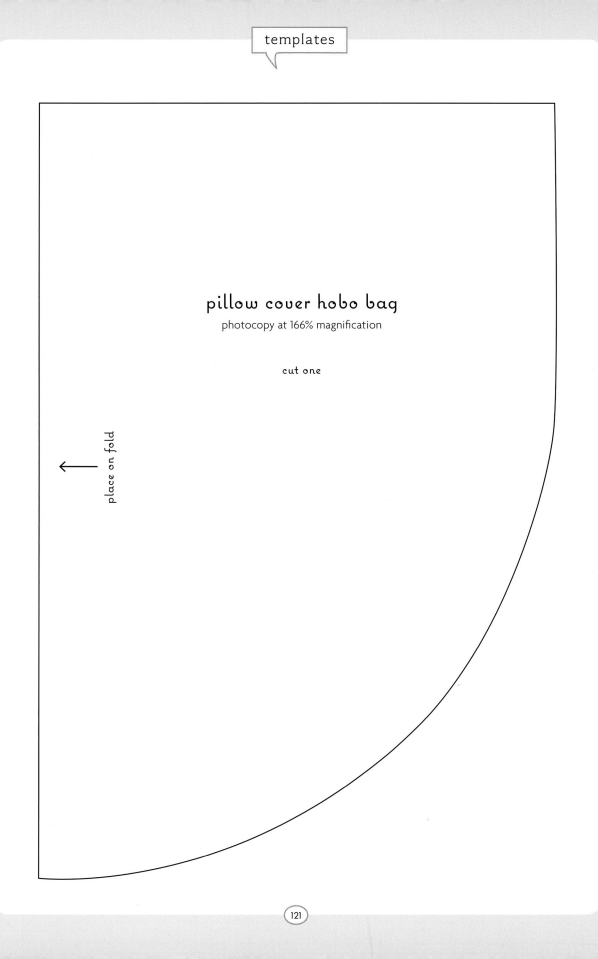

pillow cover hobo bag

photocopy at 166% magnification

cut one

place on fold

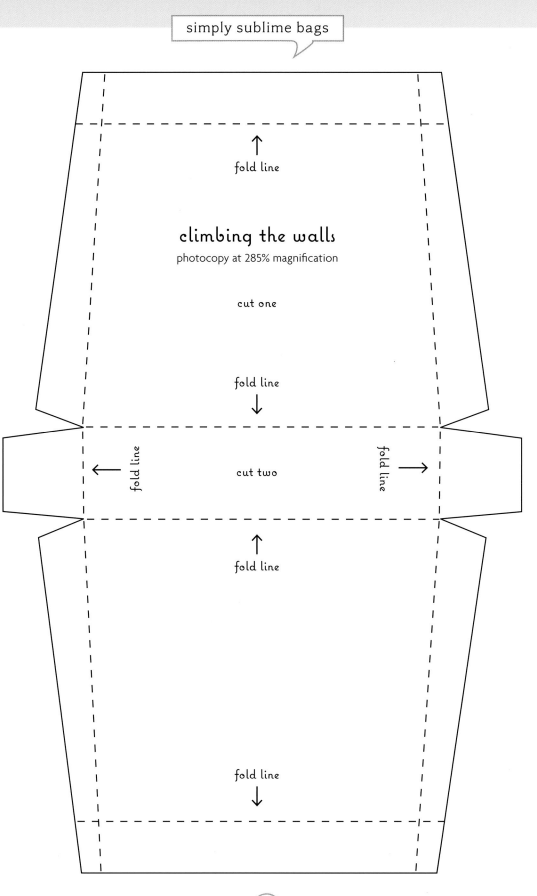

climbing the walls

photocopy at 285% magnification

cut one

fold line

fold line

fold line

fold line

cut two

fold line

fold line

campy coin purse

photocopy at 125% magnification

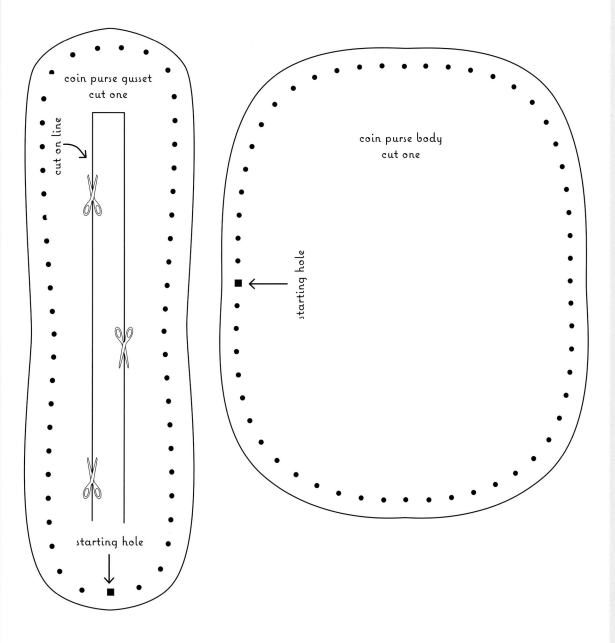

coin purse gusset
cut one

cut on line

coin purse body
cut one

starting hole

starting hole

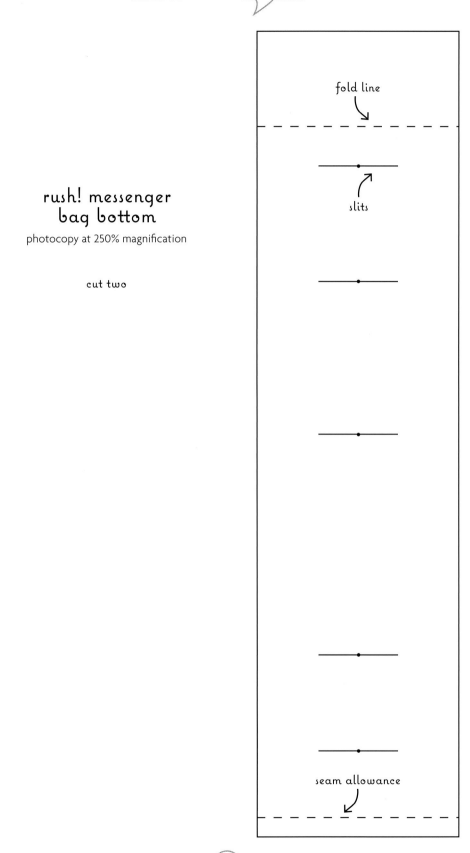

rush! messenger
bag bottom

photocopy at 250% magnification

cut two

fold line

slits

seam allowance

rush! messenger bag front
photocopy at 250% magnification

cut one front

center

rush! messenger bag back

to make bag back pattern template, photocopy bag front at 250%
magnification and extend the top edge by 17½" (43cm). keep the top
corners square. note: cut with "rush" upside down.

cut one back

acknowledgments

It took more than a village to write this book! First of all, there simply would be no *Simply Sublime* anything without my agent Andrea Barzvi. Thank you for believing in me and seeing something in me that I hadn't even seen in myself. And thank you to Rosy Ngo at Potter Craft for envisioning a bag book, and for giving me the chance to write it!

I owe so much to my incredible photographer Scott Jones. Thank you for searching for the hidden treasures and finding them, and for making the bags (and me!) look so good. And thank you to my talented illustrator Mark Watkinson, who probably makes these bags in his sleep. I love your drawings.

I could never adequately thank my "team" at Potter Craft, especially my editor, Erin Slonaker: You are more than simply sublime, you're simply amazing! And Amy Sly, my fantastic designer, you blow me away! Thanks to Chi Ling Moy, Melissa Bonventre, and Jennifer Graham for tying everything together.

A big huge thank you to all my gorgeous models, and to my generous friends who shared their homes and shops with me: Maya, Beth and Raffie Samach, Leah Doyle and Hannah and Peter Coleman, Valeria Criscione and Jon Erik Reinhardsen, Linda and Dan Volpano, Amy Frolick and Brad Scheler, Sarah, Pam and Rob Joyce, Hope Morgenstern, Jocelyn Rand, Kimberly Peters, Jane Wiesenberg, Olivia and Robin Golden, Steve Weishaus at Stan'z, Nancy Rosenberger at The Quilt Cottage, the folks at Bella Fiora and Cocoa, and the "Two Hannahs"—Hannah Lachow and Hannah Kahn.

To the girls: This book could not and would not have happened without your love, support and unwavering friendship (not too mention the carpooling, babysitting, and pep talks at all hours): Suzanne Beilenson, Eve Bercovici, Robin Bidner, Lori Cantor, Keesler Cronin, Annemarie Curnin, Linda Eisner, Emily Eldridge, Gail Greiner, Beth Kobliner, Ellen Landau, Nancy Leighton, Nora Plesent, Debi Riessen, Beth Samach, and Marian Stolman.

Thanks to my writing pals, Jill Simpson, Andi Atkins, Tamara Eberlein, Beth Levine, Ellen Parlapiano. Susan Stewart, and Louise Tutelian, for your guidance, support, and making me feel like part of the family. And to Margie Fox, Cristina Speligene, Harold Levine, and Emily Brotman for helping me get this book off the ground in the beginning.

Thank you to my pro-bono lawyer, Andy Lachow—I could never repay you, even if you had kept track of all those billable hours!

And a special thank you to my dear friend Gary Belsky for being my mentor and champion and for getting me almost every writing job I've ever had!

I would never have done anything worth writing about if it weren't for my truly amazing, generous, loving, and devoted family. Mom, Dad, Doug, Kate, your support has been my foundation. And Bette, Laurie, Sue and Dan—thank you for everything! I love you all so much.

And finally, thank you to David, Sam and Hannah for putting up with the piles, and the mess, and the bags on every doorknob of our house. Thank you for making me feel like I'm special, and making me know that I'm lucky. You are my inspiration, and even when life isn't simple or easy, you three make it sublime.

index